Smart Risks

How small grants are helping to solve
some of the world's biggest problems

Edited by
Jennifer Lentfer
and Tanya Cothran

PRACTICAL ACTION
Publishing

Practical Action Publishing Ltd
The Schumacher Centre, Bourton on Dunsmore, Rugby, Warwickshire, CV23 9QZ, UK
www.practicalactionpublishing.org

A catalogue record for this book is available from the British Library.

A catalogue record for this book has been requested from the Library of Congress.

ISBN 9781853399305 Hardback
ISBN 9781853399312 Paperback
ISBN 9781780449302 Library Ebook
ISBN 9781780449319 Ebook

Citation: Lentfer, J., and Cothran, T., (2017) Smart Risks: How small grants are helping
to solve some of the world's biggest problems, Rugby, UK: Practical Action Publishing,
<http://dx.doi.org/10.3362/9781780449302>

Since 1974, Practical Action Publishing has published and disseminated books and
information in support of international development work throughout the world.
Practical Action Publishing is a trading name of Practical Action Publishing Ltd
(Company Reg. No. 1159018), the wholly owned publishing company of Practical
Action. Practical Action Publishing trades only in support of its parent charity
objectives and any profits are covenanted back to Practical Action
(Charity Reg. No. 247257, Group VAT Registration No. 880 9924 76).

Cover photo: Momotaz Begum (pictured) lives in Mahipur, Bijor Bandh in the Rangpur
District of northwest Bangladesh. Unusually for Bangladesh, she has never married.
She says, "I have a passion for goat rearing, I love taking them around and to the fields.
Having them around me makes me happy." Photographer: Mehrab ul-Goni, Practical
Action Bangladesh

Cover design by Andrew Corbett
Typeset by vPrompt eServices, India
Printed by Hobbs the Printers Ltd, Totton, Hampshire, UK

PEFC Certified

This product is
from sustainably
managed forests
and controlled
sources

PEFC™

www.pefc.org

PEFC/16-33-415

Dedication

For Patt, for Boyd, and all those who teach us
that responsiveness is how we show love.

Smart Risks

Praise for this book

'Smart Risks is an important read for anyone who cares about poverty, inequality and social justice movements around the globe. There are many critics of global development but very few who also provide answers. The authors of Smart Risks confront the hegemonic logics of global aid that rely upon problematic assumptions about scale and outside ownership and expertise with an inspiring grounded look at how small grants, trust in local leadership, and investment in grassroots institutions promise greater and more sustainable impact in tackling some of the most pressing problems of our time.'

Erica Kohl-Arenas, Assistant Professor at The New School in New York City

'Smart Risks is a powerful reminder that local leaders are the best experts of the challenges facing their own communities, and that trusting in their knowledge and experience is the single most promising way to build lasting change. Together, these illuminating essays offer a thoughtful alternative to the pervasive and deeply misguided notion that global philanthropy and development offer silver bullet solutions to complex, deep-seated problems. Every philanthropist committed to supporting meaningful, transformative change should read this book.'

Jennifer and Peter Buffett, co-presidents, NoVo Foundation

'This book offers heartfelt, no-nonsense lessons about investing in locally led, community based initiatives for justice, equality and social change across the globe. It is never easy to take these risks, especially when seeking to keep philanthropy effective and humble across boundaries, gulfs of income inequality and diverse cultures, but in this thoughtful book, we are given reasons to recommit to engaging our resources in ways that make a lasting difference.'

Kavita Ramdas

'Smart Risks is an important and timely contribution to a conversation which finally seems to be gathering momentum. People on the receiving end of development aid invariably know what they want and need and it is rarely massive injections of money, framed in short-term projects and laced with unrealistic reporting requirements. Time and time again, small grants – disbursed with respect, without a narrow agenda and alongside other forms of support – prove their worth as a critical instrument in devolving power and resources, and in igniting the flame of local action. Read and learn.'

Jenny Hodgson, Executive Director at Global Fund for Community Foundations

Contents

Acknowledgements

Our gratitude is offered to the contributors of this book and members of the Small is Big Writing Collaborative, from whom this book was born. Thank you for your commitment to capturing and sharing our collective knowledge. Thanks to Melissa Extein and Zanele Sibanda, who worked on essays that weren't included in this volume.

We are thankful to fellow authors who offered their sage advice along the way: Marianne Elliott, Mary Fifield, Tori Hogan, Kate Otto, Alessandra Pigni, and Ruth Stark.

Those who offered critical feedback on our proposal and publishing decisions were so important to this book as it developed. Thank you James F. Brooks, Julia Callahan, Britt Ehrhardt, Sarah Ford, Nicole Lee, Kathleen Markus, Niamani Mutima, Robin Pendoley, and Mark Simpson-Vos. To our reviewers, Rachel Humphrey and Swatee Deepak, we are so grateful.

This book's final burst of energy and formatting prowess came from Angela Jia-Yin Ng. Thanks for getting us across the finish line!

Enthusiastic encouragement and feedback were deeply appreciated from: The Barefoot Guide Collective, Sandra Bass, Dayna Brown, Penelope Chester, The Coady International Institute, Victoria Dunning, Janis Foster Richardson, Sarah Hobson, Jenny Hodgson, Jane Huber, Shawn Humphrey, Chris Hufstader, Katherine Knotts, Kate Kroeger, Solome Lemma, Joop Rubens, Vuyiswa Sidzumo, and Maria J. Stephan.

We thank again and again the staff, board, partners, and supporters of Thousand Currents (formerly IDEX), Spirit in Action International, and the Oxfam America Creative Team for your investment in and commitment to demonstrating how we live our values through this book.

Our deepest gratitude to those people in these stories and around the world who are working directly – day in, day out – with their neighbors, families, and communities. Your commitment to making the world more just and sustainable fills our work with hope.

And finally to the partners, mentors, colleagues, family and friends who continually challenge our worldview, thank you.

Introduction

Jennifer Lentfer and Tanya Cothran

The essays in this book explore how personal, intentional philanthropy and investment, focused on local knowledge and close connections, can make a true and lasting impact. We share our experiences because we believe that these relationships with effective grassroots leaders, organizations, and movements are worth the risk.

Keywords: Philanthropy; indigenous organizations; international aid; aid effectiveness; community ownership

It had been a long day. Dianne slipped off her shoes after walking through the doorway. She let out a 'home sweet home' sigh as she threw the mail onto the table. It included yet another solicitation from an international children's organization to which she once donated, as well a letter from the parent-teacher association which was always active in her child's school.

Dianne flipped on the television and flopped down on the couch. The kids weren't home yet, and that was fine. Her boss has given her a new, unrealistic deadline and instead of stressing about it and working late, she had decided to just go home.

Now the newscaster was talking about yet another natural disaster in a far off island nation. So many people dead, homes destroyed. Already people had seen so much conflict 'over there'. So much suffering.

As Dianne looked around her safe and comfortable home, she felt lucky.

***

It had been a long day. Jamie was still at the office at 6:30p.m., sitting at her computer, trying to finish a report to the foundation that had given their programme a grant to support microfinance projects in three countries in Latin America.

Jamie was losing focus. She stretched and cracked her knuckles, then resumed typing again. It was easy for Jamie to lose focus these days. She did not start working for this international aid organization because she wanted to push paper. When they came back from the Peace Corps, she had been ready to change the world.

This was a report that Jamie had now written many times over, attempting to show positive 'results' to get more funding. She knew that in reality the problems that the programme was trying to address – poverty, women's empowerment, corruption – would not be solved in a year, or three years, when the grant would be finished.

***

It had been a long day. Isaac was returning home from the hospital, chatting with a friend he encountered along the road. Finally the monsoon season had come and the red dirt beneath their feet was wet and muddy.

Isaac had taken his neighbour's wife, who was having a difficult pregnancy, to the clinic on his motorbike. When they had arrived, he'd had to push hard so she could be seen by the doctor. He'd known others who had gone there, only to languish and never get the care they needed.

He left the pregnant woman once her family arrived at the clinic with food and drink, and now walked beside his motorbike. Mostly Isaac felt proud that people in his village often called upon him for help. But other times it was a burden to manage the small community group that he founded and led. His own family was far from well off.

A white sign along the road, painted with red, black, and blue letters, indicated that this was the area for yet another large internationally-funded development project. Isaac noted that the donors' logos and flags were displayed, also proudly, even though he and his neighbours had not seen any activity since the sign was installed.

***

Each one of these three people has something in common. They all believe in the ability of people to change the circumstances of their lives. They believe in the ability of people to come together to make these changes. They believe in giving to others.

Dianne, Jamie, and Isaac also have another set of common beliefs. They all recognize how resources from rich countries can be useful to people living in poverty. And they go back and forth between the optimism and the disappointment of unsustainable charitable responses to global poverty. Either through their lived experience or through the information they consume, they know the problems are bigger and more interconnected than ever before. Climate change, global inequality, broken food systems all require 'big' solutions. Don't they?

The difficulty for people engaged in anti-poverty and social justice issues across and within borders is that it's difficult to know where our resources, whether they be ten dollars or tens of millions of dollars, can be most useful. If we know helping those less fortunate than ourselves is the right thing to do, then why does it seem so hard?

All three people may be frustrated with the state of international 'aid'. But when Dianne, Jamie, and Isaac are able to fight back hopelessness, the promise remains. History has been shaped by people willing to stand up for their fellow human beings.

The good news is that the explosion of internet access, social media, and online interaction means that people want to and can be connected across boundaries. The other good news is that the distance and divisions between Dianne, Jamie, and Isaac are also shorter and smaller than ever.

But now a leap of faith is needed.

For Dianne, who cares deeply about her community and wants to act out of gratitude for her family's blessings, she will need to look beyond the 'usual players', beyond the big organizations with the marketing departments that keep her mailbox full of appeals.

For Jamie, who doesn't want to disappoint her donors and doesn't want resources to be used poorly, she will have to find the courage to do things differently and get out of the way. Her expertise will have to take a back seat to local contextual knowledge and grassroots-led initiatives.

For Isaac, whose family's welfare and personal reputation is on the line, he must risk getting people's hopes up and not fulfilling them. In many ways, Isaac has much more at risk than Dianne and Jamie. Isaac is surrounded by people struggling on a day-to-day basis. He knows the real stakes of failure.

So then how do we begin to connect all these people's hopes for the future? How do we connect the admirable efforts of these three individuals?

***

'Teach a man to fish' is the old adage that most people associate with charitable intentions. But people need to understand something different and crucial to the future of how international aid and philanthropy is offered: the man [and woman] already know[s] how to fish.

If the pole or net broke, the man would have to find the money to replace it. If the local river has been polluted, he's the one who have to find another source of water and work with local officials to clean it up. If the man fell down the bank of river and broke a leg, someone in the community would call Isaac.

It seems the stubborn, complex, and long-standing problems at the root of global poverty hold up well to the best intentions of international do-gooders. Turns out teaching a man to fish is never as 'easy' as glossy brochures or websites suggest.

***

How did the *Smart Risks* authors come together?

Many of the authors of this book have friends and relatives that are 'Dianne'. We came together because we used to be 'Jamie'. We wrote this book because we know *so* very many 'Isaacs'.

Jennifer Lentfer, creator of how-matters.org, sent out an invitation to peers and colleagues in 2011: Would they like to be part of a group of international grantmakers that would use writing as a tool for learning, and at the same time, would help demonstrate the growing relevance and impact of small grants?

Tanya Cothran of Spirit in Action International was one of the first to respond. As a team of one, Cothran was keen to connect with and learn from other grantmakers who make grants in the same way that her organization does – grants that are responsive to what community leaders said they needed on the ground, and that rely on trust rather than being driven by 'top-down' solutions.

Others soon joined the group, excited to share their ideas and grantmaking approaches with each other, and eventually, a wider audience. The group originally called themselves the *Small is Big* collaborative. They soon realized that 'small is big' didn't adequately reflect their collective knowledge. Together they represented 20 organizations and had over 125 years in international grantmaking experience. They have made approximately 12,000 grants totalling almost US$130 million to over 5,000 grassroots organizations in over 130 countries over the past 30+ years. Their work spans all geographic regions of the world and represents social change efforts in environmental protection and justice; economic development; human, indigenous, women's, and children's rights; food justice; global health; community development; transparency and accountability; and conflict mitigation and peacebuilding.

Coming together in the writing collaborative also enabled participants to see themselves as a group. As relatively small organizations, the grantmakers often operate in an isolated manner. They realized that, though their approach was unorthodox in global development, there was indeed a movement of people trying to operate in more responsive ways to everyday people.

Ultimately the group recognized the most important thing they were doing as international small grantmakers: they were taking 'smart risks'.

What's so risky about giving internationally?

When someone gives their hard-earned money to an organization, whether local or international, they naturally want to see that the money reaches the people it is intended to help. No one wants to see resources squandered. For example, if a person gives to Charity X for the Syrian refugee crisis, they want to see that those dollars fulfil Syrian refugees' immediate needs.

Getting funding to where it is to be used, however, is complicated. What's the current consensus on what works to address a given problem like a refugee crisis? Which organizations are operating on the ground? Which are doing the best work? How much oversight will there be? Are their leaders trustworthy? How much money is supporting administrative costs? How will the foreign currency be transferred? How will anyone know that the money has reached people? If the money goes towards goods and services, is this what people actually need at this time? Does it help in the long term?

These questions (just the tip of the iceberg!) can cause confusion and anxiety. People know there are many points along the chain where funds can go missing or be used unwisely. Scandals of mismanagement, when organizations fail in their responsibility to ask and answer these questions effectively, are commonly featured in the media.

One approach to limiting uncertainty in the global development sector is to design and manage projects. 'The project' is at the core of how international aid and philanthropy functions. Projects consist of setting objectives for change within a certain timeframe, and employing devoted resources to complete planned activities. Project management is widely used within the for-profit and government sectors as a means of getting things done and guarding against fraud – both important things within global development as well. Philanthropic dollars and public monies for international assistance alike are channelled through bureaucratic and high-cost mechanisms. Scholars estimate that nearly 75 per cent of US foreign assistance is given through projects, mostly implemented by US-based, for-profit contractors or through US-based non-governmental organizations (Ghani and Lockhart, 2009).

Alongside projects, the search for 'results' has become ingrained in every aspect of the international aid system as a means of minimizing risk and ensuring accountability. International organizations are making an increasing effort to find more precise ways of tracking money and measuring progress, to try to obtain more concrete answers to the question 'What works?'.

Unfortunately, as we describe below, the ways that projects are designed, managed, and evaluated in the global development sector often take decision-making power away from the people directly affected by them. This can undermine people's ability to make projects successful. Centrally-planned and -controlled short-term projects can neglect community leaders' agency and expertise, a problem long acknowledged by the aid industry.

The landscape of development in sub-Saharan Africa is strewn, for example, with construction projects by well-meaning donors that never got completed, often for lack of community participation and buy-in. Too many projects fail to take into account the knowledge, experience, and community initiatives like Isaac's group that already exist in communities. It is difficult for outsiders to have a deep understanding of the efforts that will be most effective in the long run. This means that projects' results are often limited and short-lived, and non-profits on the frontlines don't get access to the funding they so desperately need to thrive and grow.

Box 1 Local indigenous organizations

- Local indigenous organizations are defined as voluntary associations of community members that reflect the interests of a broader constituency.
- They grow out of the concern of a few motivated individuals who work together in direct response to needs within the local community, rather than being externally catalyzed.
- They spring from a sense of obligation to care for those in need, in a context characterized by inadequate or non-existent public services in resource-poor settings.
- They come into existence to mobilize locally available human, material, and financial resources – ensuring that vulnerable individuals and families are supported to receive the services they require (in most cases, these groups 'pre-date' any formal funding opportunities).
- Most importantly, local indigenous organizations are embedded in the communities they serve and are therefore well suited to assess and respond to local needs on a long-term basis, contributing to sustainable community services, development, and rights-based work.

Source: How-matters.org blog (www.how-matters.org/2010/11/08/missing-from-diy-aid-debate)

The authors see another kind of risk in large-scale humanitarian and development efforts. Too often local grassroots or indigenous organizations are either bypassed altogether, or used merely as implementing partners for plans and efforts initiated and led by people and organizations external to the communities directly impacted.

Of course, most international aid actors have a goal of working well with people and local organizations, but many barriers have made it hard to implement good intentions. Finding, funding, and supporting effective grassroots groups can still be a challenge for people like Jamie, whose first obligations are to fulfil donors' expectations and navigate the layers of bureaucracy that govern how money is spent.

What's so risky about funding at the grassroots level?

The number and diversity of civil society actors in any one country is great. Citizen-led groups that resemble parent-teacher associations, community garden projects, 'save our shore' groups, or local independent media are active in every corner of the globe. What people involved in international assistance often miss is that when nimble organizations and movements are embedded in the communities they serve, effective community leaders know best how to operate in that environment that relies on mutual responsibility and trust rather than formal accountability measures. Among grassroots groups, there are tremendous wells of untapped potential. Despite their strengths, local grassroots organizations remain on the lowest rung of the ladder of international development assistance.

Grassroots groups are often considered a liability when it comes to accountability and control. Local organizations like the one Isaac leads are viewed as having 'less capacity' by international organizations, and therefore unable to comply with the rules and procedures that come with international funding.

People don't often hear stories about organized people improving their communities in the global South or strong organizations pushing their governments to change policies that hurt poor people. Rather, the aid system is built on an assumption that outside experts have the knowledge, skills, and resources that are lacking in poor countries and communities. Also the aid system is predicated on marketing materials that show needy, desolate, and despondent individuals unable to help themselves. And so, the stories of the need for outside intervention persist, even if they little resemble what is happening in reality, in people's daily lives.

Unfortunately limited exposure to international funders' systems and expectations is a huge disadvantage for grassroots groups with good ideas. The documentation required to pass administrative muster, to submit technical proposals and reports, is a huge disadvantage. As a result, local groups are often dismissed as being chronically mismanaged, rather than being judged by their results on the ground and the potential they possess.

To large funders, small, responsive grants to local, indigenous organizations or grassroots movements may seem too difficult or expensive to administer or evaluate. Aside from accountability concerns, actors within the international aid sector often discount grantmaking at the grassroots level because of its fragmented nature. Small grants are not considered a solid foundation for the provision of regular and reliable services for citizens.

What is undeniable to the authors of this book, as a result of their decades of service, is that most families are getting by not because of sweeping international-level policies or major internationally funded programmes. Rather, those who survive and thrive do so because of the local efforts of people who organize their communities to extend support and services to families not sufficiently reached by government or international agencies.

While one grant or one group will not solve the Syrian refugee crisis or the climate crisis, small grants to effective local organizations currently remain a very small part of the picture of global development. Luckily, there is a growing number of skilled intermediary funders adept at partnering with indigenous-led grassroots groups that demonstrate solid evidence of strong community ownership within their organizational systems. The authors of this book come from this group of funders, and their experiences show that when mutual accountability is present, theft and corruption are a rare occurrence.

Old-school approaches to international aid and philanthropy miss out on the dynamism, self-determination, innovation, and voluntary resources that community groups are able to generate. Indeed, when organizations are led entirely by people from the same communities they serve, they will remain in those communities, working on these issues, long after the international agencies have left.

***

After yet another news report on an international charity's lack of effective use of resources, Dianne questions if she still really wants to give money to large aid organizations. The formerly well-known organizations just don't seem that trustworthy anymore.

Dianne's daughter's school has a very active parent-teacher association and her partner is a member of a volunteer group that refurbishes old houses in their city for poor people. The leaders of both of those organizations are really dynamic community leaders, and when she gives to these groups, she knows where the money is going. She wonders, 'Aren't there local groups in poor countries too? How could I get my support to them?'

**

Before going into the Peace Corps, Jamie went with her church group to Guatemala. There she built a home for a poor family and volunteered at an orphanage. She left money there for more homes to be built, to try to prevent families from being broken. When she returned home, however, she never heard from those community leaders again. It was so disappointing for Jamie. As she told their family after they returned, 'I just wanted to go and do *something* good for the world.'

When Jamie lived in Zimbabwe as a Peace Corps volunteer, her view of local leaders gained more nuance. Although, of course, there were some questionable characters, by and large, the people she came to know just wanted a good life for their families, and the systems of mutual support there were actually quite strong, even if people often had little to share.

In her job now, Jamie would love to fund community groups, but the people and the small, nascent organizations they knew in Zimbabwe rarely even fit the funding criteria, let alone be able to handle the administrative and reporting burden that comes with most donor funding. And even if they could find more groups like the ones they knew in Zimbabwe, which would be difficult, Jamie worried that their work would never reach the scale that most donors expected.

Jamie wondered how much of the money they saw moving around the aid system actually made it to the ground. When the Arab Spring occurred, a grassroots-up social movement having very little to do with traditional aid, it became harder and harder for Jamie to remain passionate about their job. The international aid system, they saw, no longer reflected how the world was changing around it and it didn't serve the people who they knew were working for the betterment of their communities, whether international funding was there or not. Jamie wondered often if the work they did actually made any difference at all.

**

When Isaac invited some of his friends and neighbours into his home, and asked them to join this group, he was taking a risk. He didn't yet have any money besides what little they could scrounge together as a group and from other local donations. He kept going to the internet café and writing proposals to funders he knew of or found on the web. There were so many international donor agencies and NGOs in his country, and over the years he had met some nice foreigners who seemed to have good intentions. Isaac didn't understand why groups like his could never obtain funds.

He also began building relationships with the local government officials, because they had access to some resources that could be used for the community's benefit. It was a fine line he had to walk, between saying unpopular things to the powers that be, and yet supporting their work. But he knew why he did it. He was standing with his neighbours who couldn't stand up for themselves.

His wife wished that he spent more time finding income for the family, as he did rather than for the community. To her, Isaac was ultimately risking the family's welfare.

What are smart risks?

The authors of this book are all taking smart risks by investing relatively small amounts of money in effective grassroots groups and informed, empowered leaders. Rather than following the donor-controlled, large-scale international aid funding of the past, these grantmakers find and fund local organizations and grassroots initiatives to unleash social change and innovation, led by the very people affected by our shared global challenges.

When a privileged few frame the conversation about fighting AIDS or addressing climate change, remedies are imposed from above. Those most directly impacted are excluded from the conversation. However, community responses to AIDS in rural South Africa will look very different to those in urban Thailand. Fighting for climate justice with Ottawa or Washington, DC policymakers will be different than adapting to seasonal weather-pattern changes with farmers in Uruguay. It is people on the ground who have the most important knowledge, ideas, and resources to deal with the immense and complex problems associated with global poverty and injustice in their communities – because they already are.

The 'risk' the authors take is trusting in local leadership. Circumventing the default strategy of most international aid actors means not having outsiders or Westerners determine what's right for others. They let go of control and resist the urges that lead to overbearing oversight. Rather than funding projects that they conceive and control, they learn directly from the community leaders who are social innovators in their own context, and fund their initiatives and ideas.

This risk is smart in realizing that experts and expertise are not the exclusive domain of the global North. Effective community leaders and nimble grassroots organizations know the current challenges people in the developing world face. Why wouldn't they have the best ideas for solutions? Betting on this local expertise enables the authors as grantmakers to be responsive: engaging with and listening to community leaders over time, and providing funding that directly addresses the needs on the ground. Grassroots grantmakers' engagement with their partners enables them to learn directly about what solutions are possible.

Smart risks start 'where people are', and support the local processes that build upon communities' unique strengths, resources and ideas. Smart risks also require trust in the analysis and strategies of grassroots partners and the courage and humility to accept that the best solutions often come from the ground up. Activating that potential intelligently – through financing that builds upon, rather than disrupts, existing efforts – is at the heart of taking smart risks.

Through their individual work, and through collaborating with each other, the authors realized that they have a professional – and, perhaps more importantly, a personal – resolve to share how they build upon existing human and social capital. They balance what they do know with what is knowable and take smart risks based on their assessment of the context, the community, local leadership, and proposed programmes. Taking smart risks requires a balance of due diligence, trust, and long-term perspective, as well as humility and honesty with one's self.

Along the way, the authors also realized that the proven results from their grantmaking demonstrate a profound shift in attitude and practice. People in the developing world must no longer be viewed as passive recipients on the margins of the aid industry, but as central, active leaders of their own development.

Along the way, Dianne, Jamie, and Isaac have had similar insights or clues that there are other ways to approach relationships between people in rich and poor countries. Perhaps Dianne wonders if there aren't groups like her local parent-teacher association she can directly support, rather than international organizations. Jamie might want to devote a larger portion of their project's budget to support existing grassroots efforts. Isaac would like to find more external resources to support his community-based initiatives.

Most importantly, Dianne, Jamie, and Isaac can do great things together. And today people want to be connected more than ever before. *Smart Risks* authors know the potential that can be unleashed when people are connected and are willing to build relationships; the risks become smarter.

When genuinely equitable partnerships occur, when donors invest in holistic approaches over the long term, when the people being reached are actually invested in how the money is used, when failure is defined not by how every cent is used but rather by how everyday people view the outcomes, when outsiders know how they can best be helpful and then get out of the way; the risks become smarter.

How to use this book

The chapters in this book are grouped into five parts, each focusing on an aspect of risk, as it relates to reducing poverty and empowering communities around the world. In the chapters, authors draw on their expertise and experience in the field, capturing the methods they have used for approaching and navigating the risks. The parts can be either read straight through for a comprehensive review of smart risks, or readers can skip directly to the topics that appeal to them specifically. In other words, when readers are looking to take smart risks themselves, they can pick up the book again and again depending on their particular focus.

The contributions are case studies, personal stories of lessons learned over time, provocative opinions on power and privilege, and practical frameworks for investing, measuring impact, and choosing *who*, *what*, and, perhaps most importantly, *how* to support local leaders. The authors represent a range of players within the global development sector, from grantors and funders to small-grants advocates in larger organizations, programme managers, and those who are community leaders in their own right – all united by *why* they do what they do.

Chapter overview

We begin with Part One: Investing in local expertise. Tanya Cothran exposes the critical and central role community-based organizations (CBOs) play in getting work done at the local level, though their stories are often missing from global narratives on development. Clement Dlamini of Swaziland further argues that these communities have built-in resilience mechanisms, a point often missed by international organizations. Ruairi Nolan discusses how, when working in crisis situations, local peacebuilding organizations with local knowledge and personal experience of conflict have the credibility that international organizations are unable to bring to the work. It is those with knowledge based in local realities who are the real experts, and outsiders can make a larger impact by finding, listening to, and funding people who will stay the course, argue Jennifer Lentfer and Weh Yeoh. Additionally, in taking smart risks, grantmakers can scale impact beyond the local level when leaders advocate beyond their own community to fight for lasting change in society, as Mary Fifield found in her work in Ecuador.

Smart Risk No. 2 is being non-prescriptive and flexible, with a long-term outlook. In Part Two, Rajiv Khanna discusses the importance of patience and continued engagement when partnering with a community-led organization in Rajasthan, India. Scott Fifer found he had to learn to listen for solutions, realizing that outsiders' ideas for improving a situation often do not fit with the local reality and cultural traditions. In a case study from Malawi, Cothran shares her experience of responding to a local leader *as* he was first forming an idea to improve the community. Lentfer discusses the moment she risked removing herself from decision-making on how resources were allocated, and how it allowed a stronger peer-to-peer network to emerge. Finally Caitlin Stanton argues that knowing when to risk a larger investment, after building strong partnerships, can result in longer-lasting change.

Part Three outlines Smart Risk No. 3: Looking to the grassroots for innovation. With both US and international examples, Caroline Mailloux shows how small grants for local leaders are similar to seed money for entrepreneurs. While loans with the promise of a return are attractive to international investors, Cothran demonstrates how small grants keep money and profit in a community in Malawi. A case study from Blair Glencorse finds that local entrepreneurs in Liberia are best suited to find innovative solutions for working within the system to demand citizen accountability from governments. Keely Tongate explores the necessary balance between funding both proactive and responsive action in rapidly changing contexts when partnering for the long haul. Funders can take risks and turn vulnerable moments into 'fruitful failures', as Marc Maxmeister did with GlobalGiving, and get the design right, and the costs down, before scaling up. Rajasvini Bhansali found that when trust in local knowledge is paired with flexible funding, it created space for an indigenous Guatemalan women's organization to reflect, change strategy, and create innovative solutions to deep-rooted problems.

Part Four explores Smart Risk No. 4: Rethinking accountability, and the authors explore many ways of seeking feedback beyond standard mechanisms for measuring success. Logan Cochrane and Alec Thornton explain how charity ranking tools ignore the larger context in which interventions are made, creating an overly simplified picture of what works. What looks like a potential failure can be an opportunity for community accountability, as Daniela Gusman found with her work in Uganda. Nora Lester Murad, Marc Maxmeister, and Joshua Goldstein suggest ways to design reporting that will benefit the implementing organization, as well as provide information to the funder. They discuss financial reports that recognize local contributions, SMS-based feedback, and site visits, which can all be mutually beneficial activities. Although funders often rely on rigid criteria and definable outputs, there are many valuable and relevant outcomes that cannot be quantifiably measured, argues Sasha Rabsey. Being open to step beyond the known and practicing what Lentfer calls 'rigorous humility' is a critical step in building effective partnerships and sparking lasting change.

Finally, in Part Five, with Smart Risk No. 5: Practicing vulnerability, we reflect on our role as funders, exploring the personal qualities that are essential to building the trust needed to take smart risks. Murad, who has been on both sides of the 'internationals' and 'locals' divide, demonstrates how the 'other' side in a relationship can perceive the funding process. As we deepen this understanding and build our own capacity, Lentfer writes that we must also be honest about the practices that perpetuate privilege, racism, and discrimination of all kinds in non-profits, international aid, philanthropy, social enterprise, and impact investing. As part of the Barefoot Guide Collective, Warren Feek suggests ten rules for aid professionals to help them step back from providing solutions. Another piece from the Barefoot Guide Collective poses questions for learning organizations to consider when evaluating their role in social-change movements. Bhansali shares an encouraging story from Kenya of a time when she was able to resist the temptation to serve as an 'expert'. Finally, Jennifer Astone sums up the five essential qualities of grassroots grantmakers wanting to forge effective relationships with community based organizations: curiosity, listening skills, self-awareness, openness/respect, and patience.

Who is this book for?

People who want to contribute money to changing the world have many options these days. With the landscape of 'charity' changing rapidly, people like Dianne can easily be overwhelmed by the various kinds of organizations and movements that need public support. Does she send money to the well-known international charities? What about the United Nations, or the Gates Foundation, or Amnesty International? Aren't they doing good work? And what about government's role? And corporations? Dianne also knows she can buy products now that promise to benefit people other than herself.

What about social enterprise, which seems like a good idea – businesses that have a social mission rather than a profit motive? Dianne just wants to give. How do people navigate all these seemingly different types and sizes of organizations, and their varied strategies and approaches? How does Jamie decide where to work? How does Isaac decide where to seek support?

Readers from individuals with small contributions to make, to large philanthropists and heads of international organizations with portfolios of millions to spend, can learn from the authors' experiences in this book. *Smart Risks* shines a light on what *can* be done when lasting and trusting relationships are built with the people leading the change in their neighbourhoods and nations – those who are fighting the good fight whether international funding is available or not. Though there is no one-size-fits-all or silver bullet approach to social change, this book offers insights on how to best support effective grassroots leaders, organizations, and movements around the world so that *their* grounded and strategic initiatives can reach new heights and have greater impact.

Individual donors who are seeking to become more thoughtful and intentional in their international giving without traveling around the world can use these essays to understand the ecosystem of organizations that exist outside the traditional non-profit players. It will also be useful for staff at organizations that fund or run programmes, as they talk to their board of directors and donors about the importance of focusing on smart risks. Giving circles and philanthropy groups might use it as a way to expand their focus and more intentionally invest in their vision for the world, fostering that deeper connection with the people and organizations that are pushing the world to that new place. Social entrepreneurs and impact investors who are interested in social returns, in addition to financial returns, will find that partnership can be as rewarding as presenting their own solution to an issue. Ultimately, the chapters in this book explore how personal, intentional philanthropy and investment, focused on local knowledge and close connections, can have a true and lasting impact. We share our experiences because we believe that these relationships with effective grassroots leaders, organizations, and movements are worth the risk.

The chapters are written by people willing to offer and build alternatives to 'business as usual', making room for local groups that hold great promise and potential. Anyone involved in 'donating to good causes', or even impact investing can be a part of this. Online crowdfunding platforms and the contributing authors in this book all represent new ways of thinking that are allowing everyday people to get resources directly to people, organizations, and movements in the global South.

Collectively, the authors of this book have been taking smart risks by investing in small grants to grassroots organizations that are grown from the inside and fuelled by the dedication and vision of the very people they serve for over 125 years. Organizations from small, one-person staff concerns like Spirit in Action International, to large, well-known grassroots funders like the Global Fund for Women, all focus on getting local leaders the resources that they need to address their own priorities – whether their organizations or movements are focused on human rights, conflict, disability, the girl child, food sovereignty, environmental sustainability, economic strengthening, corruption, or women's empowerment. They know how to build the trust necessary to understand, build upon, and amplify the specific strengths and contributions of local leaders, organizations, and movements. As contributor Rajasvini Bhansali says 'It requires time, patience, receptivity, and restraint'.

Regardless of our level of interest, money, expertise, length of service in the social-good sector, or the amount of bureaucracy behind us, it's time to actively explore how taking more smart risks allows us to genuinely support – not co-opt, overpower, or even quash – local initiatives.

And if everyone involved in the international aid ecosystem – including Dianne, Jamie, and Isaac – can begin to be more thoughtful and intentional in achieving direct support for local initiatives and leadership, all our efforts can reach new heights and have greater impact.

Reference

Ghani, A. and Lockhart, C. (2009) *Fixing Failed States: A Framework for Rebuilding a Fractured World*, Oxford University Press, Oxford.

About the authors

Tanya Cothran is executive administrator of Spirit in Action International <http://spiritinaction.org> in California. She lives in Toronto, Canada.

Jennifer Lentfer is director of communications at Thousand Currents (formerly International Development Exchange – IDEX) <https://www.idex.org> in Berkeley, California, although she is based in Washington DC. She was senior writer of aid effectiveness at Oxfam America from 2012 to 2015, and is the creator of the blog how-matters.org <http://www.how-matters.org>.

PART I
Smart Risk Number 1:
Investing in local expertise

Every day, around the world, citizens have the contextual expertise, past experience, and credibility to implement projects in their community. Funders and outsiders can support people to recognize their own strengths and give them space to employ them to implement lasting change at local level.

Keywords: Empowerment; peacebuilding; leadership development; disability; resilience

CHAPTER 1
Making local to global connections

Tanya Cothran

Understanding community-based organizations

'Our next proposal for your consideration is from Welfare Concern International (WCI), a local organization in Zambia.' I continued my presentation of this funding request to the Spirit in Action's board of directors with a description of the group's history, size, leadership, programmes, etc., and then I shared their current plans. 'WCI wants to build a meeting room which they can use and also rent out for additional income. They already have the piece of land to use as a building site.'

The board reacted with curiosity and puzzlement. It was not that they did not understand WCI's request. They did. It was only that they had not funded a community-based organization (CBO) before. They had many questions about how a grant to WCI might actually function.

Spirit in Action's philanthropic tradition is to fund individuals or families with small grants. Even grants that benefitted community groups, such as a training centre or workshop, were usually funnelled through an individual. As the executive administrator for Spirit in Action, a small, international, grant-giving organization, it is my job to filter grant proposals and work with applicants to hone their requests before presenting them to the board for consideration. What I saw in this request from WCI was a strong fit with other criteria for our grants; it was a self-help project and had an eye towards sustainability. I also liked that it brought together many people, not just one family, to work toward prosperity and change.

WCI is registered in Livingstone, Zambia, has its own board of trustees, and helps women in their community start income-generating activities. Unlike an individual grant request, this group already had an organizational structure, and both formal and informal recognition within the community. This increased WCI's ability to make connections and work in their context in a way that Spirit in Action International, located in California, was unable to do. In the past, WCI had received support from another California family foundation, including training in grant writing. The clear proposal, along with the modest requested amount, prompted me to bring the proposal to our board of directors. The twelve board members, most of whom were not professionals in the non-profit sector, peppered me with questions.

http://dx.doi.org/10.3362/9781780449302.001

'Why do they need administrative expenses?'

'How long have we known the organization's leader?'

'With the name, Welfare Concern *International*, is this a local organization?'

What I realized was that the questions reflected a misunderstanding about CBOs, or community-based organizations. To them, WCI was a middleman. The discussion seemed to reduce the whole of WCI to its leader, when it was clear to me that their efforts were collectively led by community members. Clearly, there was a need for deeper understanding before we proceeded with the partnership with WCI.

Probably the reason Spirit in Action's board members had a hard time initially grasping the concept of a CBO is because they don't often hear stories about organized people in Africa, or African-led organizations. NGO brochures and websites show needy, desolate, and despondent individuals, which creates a tendency to offer direct aid, such as emergency food programmes or microgrants for individuals, like the ones Spirit in Action offers.

For example, child sponsorship programmes plaster their sites with pictures of children, effectively removing evidence of the caring hand of the children's current guardians. Heifer International's famous glossy gift catalogue asks people to pick a cow, goat, or other animal to give to an individual family, though this support is offered through wider community programmes on the ground. Kiva, the microloan organization, encourages donors to choose a specific individual to give a loan to, then reveals the fact that loans are often granted by local microfinance institutions prior to being listed on the site (Karnofsky, 2011).

These approaches appeal to donors by making people feel closer to those to whom they are donating. And so, the stories persist, even if they little resemble the way that most aid actually works. Money may not be given to the individually-sponsored child, but more likely used for community-level projects that benefit many children in a village. Similarly, the cow may have been given to the family or community group before the donation is made.

Communities and local groups are not in the catalogue, but they are central to the mission of most international organizations. In fact, you don't have to look far to see that Heifer International's (2016) mission is 'to work with communities to end hunger and poverty and care for the Earth'. In narratives of global development, lost are the stories of the women's circles, church organizations, food cooperatives, collective animal husbandry groups, and self-help and savings associations that already exist to assist their members and community – even though these groups are often perfectly situated to serve the needs of the community.

Further obscuring the role of community-based groups as key community actors are newspaper articles, like the 'DIY Aid Revolution' by Nicholas Kristof (2010) of the *New York Times*, which lauds several US citizens who travel abroad to 'do good'. High praise of such social entrepreneurs perpetuates the idea that, for other places to develop, the interventions of outsiders are necessary.

Often referred to as the white-saviour narrative, this scenario plays often in the back of people's mind, consciously and unconsciously, and it feeds into their decision-making processes when they are considering how to give money.

Zambian-led CBOs simply did not fit within these traditional narratives of aid and development. We are used to hearing about international NGOs working in Africa, helping individuals. How could I further educate myself, the Spirit in Action board members, and our donors, about the role, value, and structures of CBOs? Could I shift our story to tell the work of the communities and CBOs as part of our work?

When I moved to Toronto from California, I wanted to get to know my new community. Looking to see where I might volunteer, I realized that I was surrounded by CBOs – grassroots groups of friends and neighbours coming together to better their community. Though not explicitly called 'community-based organizations', they were all around: parent-teacher associations, community garden projects, immigrant services, local independent newspapers, and more, all acting in ways that are comparable to WCI and CBOs throughout the world. I wondered if relating our local non-profits, for example the Sierra Club, to one with which the board members and donors are unfamiliar, such as an anti-female genital mutilation group called Community Initiatives for Rural Development (CIFORD) Kenya, is one way to get them comfortable with funding CBOs.

Another example is Abrigo Centre, a community organization in my neighbourhood with close ties to the community, much like WCI in Zambia. Both are using local expertise to implement projects that will help citizens and improve their communities. Also, they are able to leverage small amounts of money using passionate volunteers and local resources. Abrigo recruits volunteers who speak Portuguese to help newcomers to Canada. Similarly, WCI has volunteers who contribute their skills to train women who are starting small poultry businesses. Most importantly, both groups are better situated than outsider organizations to engage the community's support and buy-in for the work.

It was my hope that once board members and donors recognized the CBOs in their own community, it would increase their comfort with Spirit in Action International grants to CBOs in African countries and the value that they bring to the issues. Giving to a CBO and allowing them to define and implement solutions increases the independence and self-determination of the people we are serving.

So did the Spirit in Action board make the $3,000 grant to WCI to build the community hall?

They did. However, after just six months of construction, high inflation made it so that the group ran out of money to complete the building. They could not buy the rest of the supplies. While this was a real disappointment and setback, it was not a total loss. The group was able to sell back some of their unused supplies and, because of their relationship with the Livingstone City Council, they were later given an abandoned building that they were able to restore with volunteer labour.

This first grant disappointment was not enough to turn the Board away from CBOs – we know that inflation hurts organizations as much as any individual in Zambia. And though Spirit in Action International no longer chooses to support building projects, we are still enthusiastically funding CBOs.

Working through community organizations like WCI, we continually see good models of groups made up of active citizens, serving their neighbours and making life better for the people in their community. In our small way, we at Spirit in Action International are beginning to change the narrative, showing CBOs developing solutions rather than people in rich countries supporting individuals on the receiving end of charity.

Even after the grant, WCI lived on with its dedicated volunteers still organizing and serving women. And Spirit in Action's relationships with WCI lived on as well, watching and encouraging them along the way.

This year, I am bringing another WCI grant proposal to the Spirit in Action Board for their review.

Box 1.1 Where does capacity already exist?

By Jennifer Lentfer

People, under the direst of circumstances, can and do pull together. Local, indigenous organizations and grassroots movements are an expression of this solidarity. They are vital to supporting genuine, demand-driven social change that can challenge power asymmetries and address deeply-rooted inequality, injustice, and poverty. We define these groups as those that:

- are voluntary associations of community members that reflect the interests of a broader constituency;
- have grown out of the concern of a few motivated individuals who work together in direct response to needs within the community, rather than being externally catalyzed;
- have sprung from a sense of obligation to care for those in need, in a context characterized by inadequate or non-existent public services in resource-poor settings;
- come into existence to mobilize locally available human, material, and financial resources – ensuring that vulnerable individuals and families are supported to receive the services they require (in most cases, these groups pre-date formal funding opportunities); and
- are embedded in the communities they serve and are therefore well suited to assess and respond to local needs on a long-term basis, contributing to sustainable community services, rights-based work, and social transformation.

As the Grassroots Manifesto from the Global Fund for Children (2013) proclaims, 'On their own, these organizations are small, nimble, tenacious, and inspiring. They are also fragile, and burdened by the very circumstances they are fighting to transform. And their potential to change the world is worth everything we've got.'

This is why the authors of this book express a responsibility to do justice to local indigenous organizations' vast and vital efforts throughout the world. The breathtaking beauty of solidarity is found in people's belief in love as an organizing force and in the power inherent in remaining open and connected to each other as humans.

*****

Sharing ourselves

There is something equally important to having Spirit in Action's Board members understand CBOs and the local, on-the-ground reality of communities working together. It is having CBOs understand who we are as a small grant-making organization, whose usual grant amount is between $2,000 and $5,000.

I realized that CBOs and international NGOs learning about each other is a two-way street when I received a grant request for US$40,000 to build a school in Kenya. This amount may not have made a multi-million-dollar international organization bat an eye, but for us it was more than our total grants in the previous two years combined!

As a 501(c)(3),[1] Spirit in Action can technically be lumped in with a vast array of NGOs. However, rather than acting as an international NGO along the lines of World Vision or CARE International with their large operating budgets, numerous staff around the world, and national fundraising campaigns, Spirit in Action is managed by a single person (me) and a volunteer board of directors. We are funded almost entirely by donations from individuals.

In Eldoret, Kenya in 2011, a discussion with a number of our partners had brought to light the disconnect between some of their beliefs about Spirit in Action and our reality. The group of local coordinators for our Small Business Fund (US$150 microgrants to families within the communities where our coordinators live) came to me with a long list of requests. For their work, they wanted Spirit in Action to cover: motorbikes, computers, scanners, printers, building projects, and logoed t-shirts.

I realized I needed to reframe Spirit in Action's narrative within the global aid field.

After listening to their requests, I shared with them how we keep costs low. For example, we do not maintain an office space and the board shares potluck meals at our meetings. We don't own organizational vehicles or even have t-shirts. But that was not what they had seen from other NGOs in their communities. In fact, these markers were what had come to define 'good work.'

Sharing Spirit in Action's cost-conscious way of operating put me in a strong position to turn down their requests. However, as our discussion continued, we unearthed surprising similarities between the funding needs of Spirit in Action International and our CBO partners.

Just as the Small Business Fund coordinators were facing more demand for their services and were desperately seeking funds, Spirit in Action International also receives grant requests daily and must regularly turn to our donors for more support. As the coordinators put their best face forward in their applications to get grants, so too do we put our best face forward on our website and in letters to our donors. Together we are learning about evaluation and reporting.

This open discussion helped us to understand and trust each other more and to better align our priorities. On our part, Spirit in Action International agreed to send them copies of our newsletter and financial reports and to highlight and use their own words in newsletters and blog stories about them: to no longer appropriate their work as our own.

The discussion was also a moment to reconcile strains. Some coordinators seemed unsatisfied with the denial of their requests, and they shared that they had to drift towards other wage-earning opportunities outside of Spirit in Action. The board then increased their stipend to cover costs, recognizing the need there.

Our grants might be small, and our costs may be low, but the coordinators realized that it is our agile structure that allows us to be flexible. This perfectly situates us to be a supporter of community efforts, rather than implement our own programmes, which is the experience the coordinators had with other international NGOs.

There is a larger movement towards openness among aid donors and NGOs. This is seen in increasing transparency commitments, such as those which intend to release key budgetary information to citizens (Development Initiatives, 2014). Transparency and simplicity in financial reports helps partners and potential partners understand the work of the organization. Failure reports, or publically presenting failures as a way to encourage risk-taking and encourage creativity, also create a relationship of openness and truth between grantors and grantees (Engineers without Borders, 2016). If we can admit when a campaign failed or how much an event costs us, maybe our partners will also be encouraged to share when their programme does not go as intended.

The need to communicate Spirit in Action's model more openly with our partners and potential partners became apparent that day in Kenya. Most importantly, the greater understanding that developed from our discussion alerted each side to the unique role that we play in our partnership. CBOs have the ability, knowledge, and access to implement poverty-fighting programmes directly within communities. Spirit in Action International has access to donors who want to support local efforts.

Summary points

- In every country and in every community – whether rich or poor – there are groups of citizens formed to address issues in their midst.
- Current global development narratives most often portray the international actor or organization, and rarely offer recognition of the crucial role of the local CBOs they partner with to get the work done at the community level.
- Just as international actors don't fully understand CBOs, CBOs may not fully understand the reality of external organizations. Developing trust is crucial to transparent and fruitful dialogue between partners.

About the author

Tanya Cothran is executive administrator of Spirit in Action International <http://spiritinaction.org> in California, USA. She lives in Toronto, Canada.

CHAPTER 2

Community resilience: An untapped resource for sustainable development

Clement N. Dlamini

Even in the midst of perpetual poverty and adversity, there is a heart at the center of 'community' that keeps pumping through difficult times, a tenacity that sees people through. Communities are the means of survival in my country of Swaziland. Consider this:

> *James Shongwe was born with non-functioning legs in the rural community of Buhleni in the Hhohho Region of northern Swaziland. Throughout his life, James has been assisted to be mobile by his family and members of the community, who would push him around in a dilapidated wheelbarrow.*
>
> *James and whoever agreed to assist him used that same wheelbarrow to travel to and from school until James completed high school. Unfortunately, due to the lack of sufficient resources both at home and at the school he attended, James performed poorly in his Form 5 exams (final year of high school). Nonetheless, James felt he had accomplished what few people living with a disability before him had. So many people in his community had not even gotten beyond primary school.*
>
> *A church group came to Buhleni in 2009 to introduce home-based care for those infected and affected by HIV and AIDS. A committee was set up to manage the volunteer work and the community of largely semi-literate people chose James, as a person who had gone through high school, to be their leader and secretary.*
>
> *At that time, the church group fed about 70 orphaned and vulnerable children each day at a care point housed in the church sanctuary. Many of those children also received very basic reading and writing lessons there, since many could not attend school due to lack of tuition fees. It was clear, though, that the group needed income to keep the care point stocked with food.*
>
> *The children had other needs too. Those coming to the care point had very old clothes and little or no prospect of getting new ones any time soon. James' committee got together and donated money for clothes, as some unemployed women in the community had been trained to sew by an international NGO and had access to community sewing machines.*
>
> *The committee then secured a contract to provide students' uniforms and floor polish to a nearby school, the profits going to the care point. The women*

http://dx.doi.org/10.3362/9781780449302.002

also shared some of the profits, and put the money into their savings and loans association. From there, they borrowed money and started businesses to sustain themselves and their families, many having large numbers of dependents due to the impact of HIV deaths.

The women could be at the care point, while taking care of their businesses, and the community started seeing children's lives improve.

Every day, James was pushed to the care point by his family or neighbours and, in addition to his leader duties, did some of the reading and writing teaching. Seeing that it was not enough though, he and the community decided that he should go back to school. At an adult skills centre nearby, where students can enrol to upgrade subjects they had not done well in, James re-learned the subjects he had failed.

With his new skills, James returned to teach at the neighbourhood care point and, with the help of the community and the church, they started a primary school. Seeing the effort of the community, the government came to their assistance, built a fully fledged school and hired qualified teachers to teach the children. Due to a new policy of free primary school education, all the children are now able to go to school.

In 2016, the first Grade 7 (final year of primary school) class at Princess Monile Primary at Endzingeni will sit external exams. Many of the women's small businesses in the community still continue in earnest.

Started by a resilient community and driven by the passion of a resilient young man, the committee is still vibrant and going strong, dreaming of what is next for the community of Buhleni.

Am I saying communities like Buhleni don't need development interventions? Not at all. Sixty-three percent (63 per cent) of my country of Swaziland lives in poverty (UNDP, 2010). Swaziland, with a population of slightly above a million, has an unemployment rate of 40 per cent (Central Statistical Office, 2008). Current statistics reveal that of the youth that graduate with diplomas and degrees, 53 per cent are unemployed, and HIV and AIDS remains a major problem for our country's families and communities.

But I ask myself why would a country so endowed with natural resources and beautiful mountainous landscapes, and so deeply in love with its cultural heritage, linger in poverty? What is it that we are missing and not doing right? Is it really that we cannot fight the scourge of poverty? Or is it that we have not yet learned to harness our in-built community strengths?

Resilience in action today

The process of continuous survival and coping, even in the hardest of situations, is called 'resilience.' Masten (2009) defines it this way: 'Coping may result in the individual "bouncing back" to a previous state of normal functioning, or simply not showing negative effects [from shocks]'.

In sub-Saharan Africa we see the principle of resilience in action in rural and urban communities, among individuals and families, every day. Yet we have acknowledged for some time that, in the absence of a state-organized social security system, the traditional homestead has long ago ceased to offer the social safety net it once did.

Despite our continent's troubles, there is a spark of resilience that continues in the face of all these challenges. Understanding how these traditional caring systems functioned in the past is key to building a brighter future.

International actors, despite their good intentions, often miss this. For example, when people from the West think of the most vulnerable people in our society, child-headed households often come to mind. But this doesn't happen for me. I think of child-headed households as often the *most* resilient. Imagine an older sibling, single-handedly taking over the role of mother and father, providing for her or his siblings while they continue in school or finding means to protect, feed, and clothe their siblings through any means necessary. Think of the shocks that these children absorb, caused by such unexpected changes in their lives. Though engulfed by problems and assuming roles that they are not ready for, they continue to draw upon invisible, inner strength and a belief for a better future that often makes outsiders wonder, 'How do they still live on?'

When it comes to responding to such 'desperate' situations, the emergency response approach to development seems to be our main undoing. We run around fighting fires, rather than making means for citizens to stand on their own to prevent or stop these fires. Unfortunately, this firefighting approach is the very thing that entrenches vulnerability. The cycle keeps repeating itself.

Rather than being bogged down by vulnerability, we need to start focusing on community strengths. Communities have in-built resilience mechanisms to help minimize the effects of disruption and disorder caused by the many social problems in an entire society. These are established on shared values and humane systems of mutual support.

There is no school of resilience people can attend. Rather, people discover it when their lives are stretched beyond their limits. It cannot be imported. Resilience is an inherent gift of humankind.

Are typical development interventions at odds with resilience?

Self-organization is the willingness and drive that pushes an individual, family and community to graduate from the margins of society to a place of self sustainability. It cannot be denied that human beings have ways of responding to struggles in their lives in the absence of external partners like donors.

Throughout my career in social work, I have watched with interest as civil society (myself included) designed activities together with communities, which, we believed, would pull communities out of the cycle of poverty and mediocrity. Some interventions worked wonders and have led to communities continuing to sustain themselves and improve their livelihoods.

But, unfortunately, this is not the norm. Most interventions are designed on behalf of communities, based on 'best practices' or cut-and-paste, one-size-fits-all solutions that disregard the uniqueness of environments, communities, or individuals. Interventions also end as soon as the international donor pulls out. Then activities begin to slow down and people return to vulnerability.

In social work we employ personal empowerment and systems approaches in the intervention process. The personal empowerment approach recognises that individuals have internal strengths and potential, and in times of struggle they can draw on these strengths rather than rely on external influences. The systems approach acknowledges that we are all shaped by our environment and the people that surround us. Our families are the first systems that influence our life. If someone grows up in a family of abuse then they learn those practices. But when they move outside of the family environment there are many others who can influence the person and help them 'unlearn' the abusive behaviour. They are part of many systems – community, church, school, career, friends – that can all combine to influence their life. This approach has lessons for smart risks in sustainable development. Building on people's personal, internal strengths requires a shift in mindset; being willing to integrate the views of communities, rather than continue to marginalize them.

From where I stand, typical development interventions are more donor driven, and less about the lived realities of the people we are serving. In effect, we forget *who* really matters. If we push an agenda from our perspective and forget that communities have survived and continue to survive in spite of our efforts, then we are bound to fail.

Meaningful consultation with communities must become a 'must-have'

Taking smart risks with communities requires asking ourselves what is really the change that we want to see during and after an intervention, project or programme ... *beyond* outputs. And there is no way we can ask this question and get an answer without proper consultation with community members.

Often the argument of practitioners against consultation is that the cost is too high. However, the cost of consultation versus the cost of an ineffective programme means its long-term dividends cannot be overlooked.

Properly consulting communities is banking on the fact that communities are smart risks. In many places, you can be leaders of a resilient lot that will survive, even without interventions. A lesson I have learnt from my work is that development is already inherent in community systems – communities know what they need and what to do to come out of their poverty situation. They simply lack resources and technical know-how.

So, as outsiders coming into their systems, we need to develop a mentality of appreciating who people are and the resilience they employ, rather than just disrupting the way they do things with short-term interventions.

At the heart of resilience is an underlying drive for human beings to sustain themselves and move forward in their lives. It is internal strength that pushes communities to fight for survival and push for development.

The question that remains for us all is how do we better leverage these strengths?

Summary points

- Communities have in-built resilience mechanisms, established on shared values and humane systems of mutual support.
- International efforts miss this. For example, child-headed households are usually viewed only as vulnerable. Consider how child-headed households could also be seen as the most resilient.
- Taking smart risks with communities requires recognizing that individuals have internal strengths and potential they draw upon, and recognizing that different approaches to international partnership are needed to build upon communities' and people's strengths.

About the author

Clement N. Dlamini, MSW, is a social work lecturer at the University of Swaziland. He was head of the Department of Public Health Management and head of training and student affairs at the Institute of Development Management in Swaziland between 2011 and 2015.

CHAPTER 3
Peace begins at home

Ruairi Nolan

Pakistan has a notably rich civil society. A new staff member at a leading European donor in Pakistan, herself a Pakistani, contacted my organization a few years ago. She was deeply aware of the complexities of the conflicts in her country and she wanted to find ways to support civil society to counter the threats that her country faced.

Yet she had also found that her donor agency, led by international staff on short-term postings, was so caught up in the latest crises that they lacked the institutional memory and systems to properly engage with Pakistani civil society. Instead, her agency worked with the same old faces', a select group of entrenched partners who knew the donor systems. She was frustrated that she could not branch out and take the sort of calculated risks that would allow the donor to really make a difference.

The security situation in Pakistan and the restrictive security policies of donors mean that many cannot visit grassroots organizations in their home locations. Consequently, donors tend to form the strongest relationships with larger groups who can afford to have a presence in the capital, Islamabad. Unfortunately, even where individuals within large institutions can be persuaded of the importance of local groups, oftentimes they are hamstrung by the practices and structures of their organizations. In Box 3.1, we highlight some of the blockages that prevent funding structures that are supportive of local groups.

We consulted various grassroots civil society groups in Pakistan and they told us the same story, though from the other side. Everyone knew who the key international donors were but, for smaller groups, it was difficult or impossible to get a meeting with them, never mind a partnership. I heard from many people variations of the joke that 'Islamabad is really 20 miles from Pakistan', emphasizing the gap between life in the relatively wealthy and international capital, and life in the rest of the country.

This example illustrates how interest in the work of local groups did not translate into enough practical support for their work. We decided to partner with some local groups to arrange a conference to try and address this problem. We convened local peacebuilding organizations from across Pakistan to share knowledge and expertise, plan joint projects, and to meet with donor agencies based in the capital city.

http://dx.doi.org/10.3362/9781780449302.003

Box 3.1 Why doesn't the international community invest in local peacemakers?

Peace Direct identified the following blockages in the peacebuilding sector that offer clues as to why international funders do not put local initiatives first in conflict and post-conflict settings:

1. The international community is not aware of who the local peacebuilders are.

Many agencies understandably find it difficult to identify credible local peacebuilders, especially in areas that are conflict-prone and inaccessible to outsiders. This leads to a tendency to engage with only a very narrow section of civil society that normally has a presence in major towns, or for outsiders to make decisions themselves.

2. Funding structures are not suitable for supporting local peacebuilders.

The majority of donors are unable to administer the small grants that are needed to support local peacebuilders because they are:

- typically impatient to see impact with short-term commitments;
- reluctant to provide core funding; and
- tend to be slow to release funds.

   The policies of some large donors recall Mark Twain's famous quip, 'I didn't have time to write a short letter, so I wrote a long one instead.' Lacking the time and resources to offer small grants, instead they choose to disburse their funding in large tranches that effectively rule out the groups with the closest connections to their communities.

3. Local peacebuilders are not given status by the international community.

Most international agencies include community involvement in their mandates and policies, but in reality local peacebuilders are rarely given a place at the decision-making table and sometimes not even consulted. In part, this is a lack of awareness of what local peacebuilders achieve, but it is also an attitude that struggles to relate to grassroots organizations, which may have less formally-recognized structures.

4. Most agencies are not willing to take the risk of working with small unknown organizations.

Agencies tend to favour organizations that have a reputation and a history of working with the international community. Small organizations may require additional support in reporting, including on finances, and donors are reluctant to make sufficient allowances for this. This does not encourage new talent, and tends to lead to large capital-city based 'local' NGOs that mimic INGOs and lose the very 'rootedness' which is key to their success.

At the conference, there was a divide between representatives of those Pakistani organisations headquartered in Islamabad and those who had travelled from parts of the country most affected by conflict, such as Federally Administered Tribal Areas (FATA), Khyber Pakhtunkhwa and Balochistan. The groups from Islamabad, often staffed by internationally-educated people, were well versed in working with donors and were fluent in much of the jargon and technical language so common in development work. They were better able to mix with the international donors and make the sort of sharp 'elevator pitch' that can be so important. The groups based in the most conflict-affected regions clearly did not have the same knowledge of how the donor system works, even if their work on the ground was of very high quality.

After the event, the donors told us that they were very impressed by the quality of analysis and the presentations of the local peacebuilding groups.

However, later follow up after the event indicated that, whilst there was increased collaboration amongst the civil society groups, there were few new partnerships with the international donors.

Why was this? Many international donor organizations are full of dedicated, thoughtful staff who want to find ways to collaborate with local civil society. However, despite this, many of them still find it difficult to shift and adapt the way they work to properly accommodate and support local organizations. From our experience at Peace Direct, we know that the funding situation for local groups in Pakistan is not unique. There are many countries where international aid funding remains concentrated in organizations based in the capital city.

Why local leadership matters

When donors have difficulties in reaching out to community-based peace-building organizations, this has serious consequences. Good local peacebuilding work is based upon deep knowledge of social contexts, culture and languages. It requires long-term, patient investment in activities at a community level that build trust and dialogue, bring together enemies or combatants, and advocate for the rights of citizens.

Another example in the Democratic Republic of Congo (DRC) illustrates the strengths and importance of local leadership in peacebuilding. The *Centre de Résolution des Conflits* (CRC) was founded in Nyankunde in 1993 by Ben and Kongosi Mussanzi, a husband and wife. As tribal tensions rose in their community, Ben was nearly killed by in a violent attack because of his tribal identity. The experience made him swear to work for cohesion in his community.

Twice in its first decade, the staff had to flee for their lives, as war broke out in DRC. First, they fled to nearby Bunia, then more than 500 km on foot to Beni. One of CRC's directors was killed along with his wife and two-week-old child. Its co-founders then had to flee the country, and its offices in Nyankunde and Bunia were ransacked and destroyed.

From the beginning, CRC knew that their success would be based on the quality of their links within communities.

'The main thing is to start with grassroots people', explains co-founder Kongosi. 'When we used to talk with people, we used to give the example of a river, and if the river is polluted, you can't start if it is polluted from the source. You can't say "now we are here, let us start working here". You have to go to the source, and from there, you go slowly down the river. And thus peace means starting with the grassroots, dealing with the people who are living the impact of the conflict.'

In its early days, CRC was an all-volunteer organization. Its staff included former combatants, and all had personal experiences of the costs of conflict. This personal experience of conflict gives the organization credibility when working with people and communities in eastern DRC that no international organization can have. CRC's knowledge of peace and conflict is not theoretical; the organization's strategies and techniques have been developed and honed locally through trial and error, and applied even as killing was taking place around them. Religious faith has given them strength to carry out this work and remains an integral part of what they do today.

Since those early days, listening to the community and following their lead has meant the CRC has undertaken a wide range of programmes, reflecting the different impacts the conflict in DRC has had on the population. It has also allowed them to grow and reach more people every year. For example, in 2015, CRC established 19 agricultural cooperatives, supporting 559 people to develop investment plans for their farms. They arranged 180 microloans and training to support their socio-economic recovery. All programmes have been developed according to the priorities identified by the communities where the CRC is based.

While doing all this, they also helped release 100 child soldiers from militia groups. The work in the release of child soldiers, as part of the CRC's disarmament, demobilisation and reintegration (DDR) programme, in particular highlights the importance of local leadership. The trust that the CRC has built up at community level allows it to act as a key link between communities, local government, militia groups, and the international community. This trust and credibility is vital to the ability of the CRC to negotiate the return of child soldiers. Compared to large-scale programmes of international actors (such as MONUSCO, the UN mission in DRC), the CRC places more emphasis on the reintegration element, ensuring that when combatants leave militia groups both they and the host communities have the support needed to ensure they don't return to the bush to fight again.

The CRC focuses strongly on ex-combatants and vulnerable women, but also draws on the volunteer capacity of the community to support their programmes. Residents have been supportive because they see the benefits of the programme for the community. The community also knows that the CRC will remain there working on these issues long after the international groups and UN have left the country.

The effectiveness of the programme has led to the CRC being recognised by MONUSCO, which has consulted with CRC on how to improve their own programmes. CRC is working to help share their learning with the international community.

Too often, local organizations like CRC are either bypassed altogether by the international community, or used merely as implementing partners for the plans of outsiders. This misses out on the dynamism, innovation and voluntary resources that community groups are able to generate.

Why risk working with local peacebuilding groups?

My organization, Peace Direct, builds relationships with organizations like CRC in order to support work that is genuinely locally led. We offer small grants that cover organizations' core costs. This means funding that can be used towards the running costs of the organization (usually, rent, salaries and travel costs), or allocated to other activities as needed. This flexibility

Box 3.2 Four steps to more (and better) support to local civil society

The *Local First* campaign promotes an approach to development that looks first for the capacity within countries before bringing in external expertise and resources. Peace Direct joined forces with other organizations to launch the campaign to persuade people *why* it is important to support smaller, locally led initiatives. It also attempts to address the question of *how* this can be done through research into different models of locally led development (Peace Direct, 2014). The following strategies have been identified:

1. Identify and support local capacity

Before starting new programmes, funders and international partners should do a detailed assessment of what capacity exists in the area they want to work in. They shouldn't limit their focus to who has the capacity to immediately deliver programmes, but instead focus on creating support for local capacity to grow and sustain itself without international support.

2. Listen to local voices to develop responses and approaches

More time and resources should be spent listening to communities and local partners. Although many funders do carry out 'community consultations', the *Listening Project* demonstrated how these were often felt to be tokenistic by host communities (Anderson et al., 2012).[2] More flexible and participatory mechanisms should be used, to ensure that communities feel that they are respected and valued. Furthermore, good-quality consultations make it more likely that programmes are delivering what is really needed. The practice of listening to communities should not just happen at the beginning of projects, but there should be continuous feedback mechanisms.

3. Use funding mechanisms that support (not distort) local civil society

Much donor funding is distributed in large tranches, through processes that are not accessible to local groups, and when funding does arrive it can distort the way local civil society functions. Funding should be at levels that are consistent with the pace of change at community level. Funding should include core support to organizations to allow them to develop their overall effectiveness, not just implement more activities. It should also be flexible to allow organizations to adapt as the situation changes, making the most of their expertise in the context.

Large donors struggle with smaller grants, but carefully designed funding mechanisms can overcome these obstacles. That can be, for example, through intermediary mechanisms, where different donors come together to pool their funding. This can allow for decentralising the funding structure, greater local leadership in how the pooled funds are allocated, and better relationships with the grantees.

4. Supporting local actors to work together to achieve greater impact

Foreign aid is often criticised for encouraging competition rather than collaboration. When competition for funding pits organizations against each other, the potential for collective action can be destroyed. With the aim of achieving broad social change, international agencies often attempt to promote collaboration and reduce competition through facilitating networks of local actors. However, supporting networks does not come without its own set of problems and challenges. Networks are notoriously unstable and marked by complex power dynamics. Fluidity and adaptability are part of their strength, but the role of external support in this context must be equally flexible and responsive to changing contexts and power relations. External support should position itself so that it is able to respond to opportunities when they arise, in line with the wider social context.

is particularly important for peacebuilding organizations, who are almost always working in complex and fast-moving environments.

This also means the local organization carries out work according to *their own* strategy and priorities. Placing trust in our partners as they decide how to use the funds is vitally important. As one Nepali partner once told us, '£100 from Peace Direct that I can use with my discretion is worth £100,000 to deliver a donor's project.' This is because when local organizations have the opportunity to design their own programmes, in accordance with the needs of the community, they are much more likely to be effective and to have the most lasting impact.

Although we start partnerships with small, often nascent local organizations, our aim is to develop long-term relationships that allow the organizations to grow what they do, reaching more people and having deeper impacts, according to long-term goals which people have collectively identified.

We put an emphasis on helping partners to grow at an appropriate speed. Too much funding too soon can actually be damaging to local organizations or grassroots movements. Funding can introduce rivalries over the funds, and create a separation between the organization and the local community, reducing the volunteer basis on which they depend for their success. The funding can also reduce the accountability that the organization feels. Rather than being accountable to the community, they can instead start feeling primarily the need to be accountable to the funder.

For this reason, Peace Direct does not just think that it is important to get *more* funding to community groups. It is equally important to get the *right* funding to the groups. The challenge is to provide the sort of funding and support that allows groups to determine their own strategies for peacebuilding and development. By supporting local peacebuilders in a way that helps them grow along their own path to peace and development, genuinely local, effective grassroots-led approaches emerge.

Summary points

- Peacebuilding especially requires people who know the conflict and local context. Personal experience of conflict gives local peacebuilding organizations credibility that no international organization can bring to this work.
- Peacebuilding requires long-term, patient investment in activities at a community level that build trust and dialogue.
- Taking smart risks with local CBOs then asks for flexibility as local partners are working in complex and fast moving environments.

About the author

Ruairi Nolan is head of research and engagement at Peace Direct <http://www.peacedirect.org> in London, UK where he manages the *Insight on Conflict* publication and coordinates the *Tomorrow's Peacebuilders* competition.

CHAPTER 4

Dedication, incentives, and what drives local leaders

Weh Yeoh

This is the story of Phearom. She is my hero and one of the reasons why I still believe that we can do great things in global development.

This is what Phearom's day looks like. She travels by motorbike to her non-profit organization's small office, just outside Siem Reap, Cambodia. It's over 35°C/95°F already, but the office doesn't have air conditioning – only a few fans to keep the staff cool. She brings a small blue water bottle from home, because they can't afford a water cooler. It has a thin strap that goes around her wrist, to prevent her from leaving it behind. After some planning with her team members, she gets back on the motorbike and travels for an hour to meet twelve-year-old Ouk Ling.

Ling has cerebral palsy – brain damage that occurs around the time of birth. As a result, his movement is affected and his speech is slurred. He's intelligent and affectionate. In fact, when I accompany Phearom to see him, he bursts into a huge smile and runs towards her to give her a big hug. Since Phearom has been visiting him, transformational change has occurred in Ling's life. Previously, people had difficulty understanding him, even when he said his own name. Thanks to Phearom's work, he can now communicate in basic sentences with those around him.

Not only that but, at the age of twelve, Ling started going to school for the first time. Phearom worked with Ling's teachers to help them understand his disability and be more patient with him. Once living in isolation and being unable to communicate with those around him, Ling now jokes that he has 'too many friends'. Ling is not just participating at school, he's excelling. He is second in his class.

Phearom travels an average of 70 km (43 miles) every day to the homes of any number of the 36 children with disabilities on her caseload. This means in the almost ten years she has been working with her organization, Capacity Building for Disability Cooperation (CABDICO), she has travelled the equivalent of the circumference of the earth more than twice.

She is of the age where most Cambodian women are married and having children. Recently, her mother tried to arrange for her to be married to a local businessman, which would have meant quitting her job and helping him with his business. Phearom refused.

http://dx.doi.org/10.3362/9781780449302.004

'If this man really loved me, why would he stop me from doing the thing that I love the most?' she asks. 'Often in Cambodia, people don't think that women can work in different fields. So, I am even prouder to be a woman working in this job.'

As one of very few people in Cambodia with practical and immediately-applicable knowledge of how to improve the lives of children with disabilities, Phearom is very much in demand. Recently, a better-funded organization offered her a job that would double her $200-per-month salary. Phearom turned it down.

To begin to understand why she did this is to begin to understand the struggle to find resources that organizations like Phearom's face. Even though Phearom has plenty of experience working with children with disabilities, there is one key area of knowledge that needs to be strengthened – speech therapy. Speech therapy is a profession that helps people who have difficulty communicating, or eating and drinking, safely. In the US, there are over 130,000 speech therapists, yet in Cambodia, there is not one Cambodian university-trained speech therapist.

Phearom estimates that up to 70 per cent of the children she sees have problems with communication, while up to 60 per cent cannot swallow food and liquid safely. The latter can cause pneumonia and often death. In fact, at least two children that Phearom visited have died in this manner. She describes how one of them literally choked to death on his own phlegm because his swallow was not strong enough to allow it safe passage into his stomach. This weighs heavily on Phearom.

Phearom's organization, however, realized the importance of speech therapy for the children and families they support. They found speech therapy was not included in international donors' disability funding priorities and there is no particular fund in the world to develop speech therapy as a profession. They were instead trapped in the cycle of doing the kind of work that typical donors had identified as important.

But what if we could find a way to show others, including donors, that speech therapy works in Cambodia? Through crowdfunding, we raised enough to start a pilot project in Cambodia. We used the funds to develop the speech-therapy skills of Phearom and other team members.

'Before, I was not clear how to work with children with communication and swallowing problems, but when I had training in speech therapy, it made it easier for me to make decisions on my therapy', she tells me. 'I refused the job [with a better-funded organization] that paid more because I have had the opportunity to learn about speech therapy. That convinced me to stay.'

What I see with Phearom is the ultimate dream of living one's life's purpose, and the dream of development – Cambodian people helping Cambodian people. Surely, this is what global development should be all about. And yet, very often, the international aid system and global philanthropists, social entrepreneurs, and impact investors don't support everyday people like Phearom, who are reading the local conditions and devising their own fixes, solutions, and innovations.

I have learned that that if I listen to people like Phearom, truly listen, I can learn what the real priorities in countries like Cambodia are. Despite the half a billion dollars of aid money flowing in Cambodia, and thousands of non-profit organizations, it is people like Phearom that can see problems, and can dedicate themselves to addressing them effectively.

Our role as outsiders should be to help people like Phearom do their jobs better, to ensure they have the resources to be effective, and to think about the entire ecosystem in which they work. Organizations like CADBICO take smart risks every day, when, because of their mission and the people they serve, they see and develop solutions outside of funder priorities. There are so many more people like Phearom in the world, willing to sacrifice and commit their lives to improving their communities.

Invest in people like Phearom and great things can, and will, happen.

Box 4.1 Three key strengths of grassroots organizations

By Jennifer Lentfer

1. Contextual expertise – As locally-rooted institutions, grassroots organizations have vital expertise in the interpersonal and caring relationships in a person's everyday life. Their day-to-day interactions with marginalized people and their families, along with language and cultural skills, allow grassroots organizations a deeper understanding of how people cope, and the social fabric surrounding them, than any other social good actor. This intimate position within people's lives and in the community enables grassroots organizations to: (1) have the legitimacy and trust to reach marginalized and isolated people with supportive and appropriate care; (2) design programs and campaigns that are deemed most necessary and sensible in their locality; and (3) use their expertise to influence local support systems and institutions (e.g. families, schools, etc.) to more adequately fulfil people's rights.

2. Continuity – Large development projects led by governments, international aid agencies, and foundations reach people, but they often come with a narrow focus, restrictions on how the funding can be used, and fixed timeframes. However, grassroots organizations have the direct and lasting relationships needed to support a people throughout their life journeys. Grassroots organizations staff and volunteers often know the people and families they serve on a one-on-one basis, resulting in a very personal stake and a long-term commitment to the success of their efforts to ignite people power.

3. Connectedness – Embedded in the community, grassroots organizations can help marginalized people develop a genuine sense of belonging, self-esteem, leadership, and ownership that enables them to expand their intimate circles of support. Those who have connections to each other and beyond their own families are healthier, physically and mentally, and are more able and willing to make positive changes in their lives.

Despite these competencies, grassroots groups face a formidable challenge; they must continually seek out and compete for new resources in a funding environment that is often led by global trends rather than persistent, ongoing challenges, and that favours short-term grants to larger, higher profile, groups. Yet effective grassroots organizations are continually overwhelmed with community demand for their programmes. Grassroots groups are there, directly working with people, whether outside support is available or not.

Summary points

- Donor priorities aren't always the same as local priorities. Organizations struggle to find funding when the communities' priorities differ from those of donors.
- Effective leaders look at the whole ecosystem of their problem when they develop solutions.
- Dedicated people are motivated by more than money. Outsiders can make a larger impact by finding and funding people who will stay the course.

About the author

Weh Yeoh is founder and managing director of OIC Cambodia <http://www.oiccambodia.org>. He co-founded the blog whydev.org <http://www.whydev.org/> in 2010.

CHAPTER 5

The real experts

Jennifer Lentfer

The first and most challenging exercise of the day required me to fill in the following blanks, and then share with the group of strangers assembled by The OpEd Project:

Hello, my name is _____.
I am an expert in _____.
I am expert because _____.

I struggled. I wasn't the only one. Every other person in the room (mostly women, a few men of colour) who was participating in the seminar on thought leadership that day struggled. All of them, who were highly accomplished in their fields – heads of organizations, accomplished academics, business owners – fumbled over their words, made caveat after caveat, apologizing for what they *know*!

Many of us have trouble claiming our 'expertise' in any one area, let alone claiming our voice, our space, or our rights. But who doesn't? In the US, for example, most of the 'expert' voices we hear in the media are from an extremely narrow group – mostly western, white, privileged, Christian, and overwhelmingly male.

This certainly happens in the fields of international aid and philanthropy as well. Power, prestige, expertise, and information is concentrated within the do-gooder 'industry' around those with resources. And it greatly shapes the people from whom we hear and whom we expect to hear when it comes to fighting global poverty, i.e. *not* the people most affected by it. Consider the example shared in Box 5.1 by Smart Risks contributor Clement Dhlamini from Swaziland.

I live in Washington, DC, right next to the city's three-block-wide convention centre. The first conference I attended there was in 2012. An estimated 25,000 participants from more than 185 countries assembled there for the XIX International AIDS Conference. I couldn't help but wonder, of those 25,000 experts, how many had first-hand experience of dealing with HIV and AIDS care in a poor country? How many of them have cared for a dying neighbour, or comforted a grieving child? How many have actual on-the-ground expertise like Saeed Wame in Malawi?

Saeed Wame grew up as an orphan. He owned his first pair of shoes at age 12, and with the support of extended family and friends, he received an

http://dx.doi.org/10.3362/9781780449302.005

Box 5.1 The engineer and the elderly man

By Clement Dhlamini

During my tenure at a large international NGO, this story was told of a community garden they funded in the community of Nkwene in the Shiselweni Region, in the southern part of Swaziland. The members of the garden project requested support from the international NGO for an earth dam. This structure was meant to be a catchment for harvested water from the nearest mountain to feed the garden, which was located at the foot of the mountain.

So, as was the culture of the organization, the international NGO sought out the services of a professional, an engineer, from the neighbouring Republic of South Africa to come and determine the specifications of the proposed earth dam, i.e. its depth, proximity to the source of the water (the mountain), and the final location. After the specialist engineer was done with his scoping and analysis, the community was invited to a meeting where the engineer was to present his recommendations.

After the engineer finished his presentation, one elderly man spoke up. He was not convinced that the engineer had chosen the right location for the earth dam. The village elder worried especially about the dam's proximity to the water source, that it would cause seepage under the dam as time went on, and that water would eventually not be collected as intended.

The engineer was upset because he felt the old man was undermining him, and the international NGO overruled the old man due to his lack of engineering expertise and went with the engineer's recommendation. The earth dam was dug, water was harvested, and everyone was happy. That was, until the dam started losing water to seepage, just as the old man had predicted. The engineer had been paid and had left, so the problem remained with the community. Soon the earth dam dried up completely.

The old man was right. The engineer and the international NGO had failed to appreciate the knowledge of someone who had lived all of his life in Nkwene. The man had massive agricultural experience in the area. His recommendation, offered without a degree or professional legitimacy, but with contextual wisdom, had been right.

---

education. As the AIDS pandemic swept across Malawi, he saw many orphans struggling in his home area of Namwera and was called to help. Saeed had more than a passion, or even a vision for change. Because of his own personal history, he had a deep understanding of what might be most beneficial to orphans.

'Why was I called to do what I do? Because other people had to help me to be where I am today. It was like they were planting a tree. I want to do the same', Saeed says.

What is undeniable to me, after my decade of service in the HIV sector in Africa, is that most families do not get by because of sweeping national-level policy protections or major internationally-funded programmes. Rather, those who survive and thrive do so because of the local efforts of people who organize their communities to extend support and services to families not sufficiently reached by government or international agencies.

I met Saeed in 2005. He had founded the Namwera AIDS Coordinating Committee (NACC) in 1996 with zero dollars and a vision for a brighter future for children like himself. Today NACC is operating in 400+ villages in four districts in southern Malawi, serving over 11,000 children and their families, with a budget of over $100,000. NACC has gone from strength to strength, adding holistic programmes and deepening its presence in the community with HIV prevention and care, maternal health, early childhood development, and education. NACC's approach is to work with the community to analyse the root causes of problems locally and then explore solutions together. 'We don't plan in the office and then go to the community and say, "do this". It's not like that', says Saeed.

In education, NACC is not about just getting kids in school. Rather, it assists community members to assess and analyse the barriers to attendance, performance and completion, and their root causes. For example, a village NACC supported in 2011 identified distance as a major obstacle to primary school access; 7 km was too far, especially for younger children. NACC facilitated the community's meeting with invited local Ministry of Education officials, in which the community offered to build a junior primary school for lower grades, if the government could supply the teachers. And that is what happened.

Be it child labour or property-grabbing cases, NACC uses the same problem-solving approach, especially where culture and laws are in conflict. For example, 12-year-old 'Hawa'[3] had passed her exams to get into secondary school, but was forced into marriage by her family instead. When NACC's volunteers found out about the situation, they intervened. The girl's mother then appeared in NACC's offices, seeking not only assistance, but redemption.

'She cried that she wanted forgiveness. She said she didn't know there were laws', says Saeed. He told her that forgiveness would come when she took her child away from the new husband, which she did. Hawa then went on to secondary school and became an active NACC volunteer who 'encourages her friends to work hard at school and not rush for marriages.'

These are the intimate, personal, and family issues at the community level that local organizations are best placed to address. Saeed explains, as staff member of a local organization, 'We experience these kinds of issues day-to-day ourselves. Therefore it is we who can help discuss with community members and officials with a way to address the problems *together.*'

Not only that, the story of this 12-year-old girl retrieved from her early marriage travels. It may only be one case, one 'result' in terms of what NACC is able to accomplish, but it gets people talking.

'Other families now think twice before they marry off their young daughters. It may be only one story, but it has real impact,' Saeed explains. 'Yes, [early marriage] is in our culture, but people learn from each other that it is against ourselves.'

This kind of expertise – the sharing of context and experience and mutual support – is what has enabled Saeed to transform his community over the past 20 years. In the case of the fight against HIV and AIDS, the knowledge and local efforts of people like Saeed Wame are invaluable. I wonder how he would answer the questions:

Hello, my name is _____*.*
I am an expert in _____*.*
I am expert because _____*.*

While Saeed has now been invited to attend some international AIDS conferences, it's exactly his kind of expertise that is too often missing from the discourse about fighting global poverty. It is exactly Saeed's kind of expertise that makes him a smart risk.

And there are plenty of experts to choose from. Malawi's National Aids Commission identified over 1,100 community-level initiatives for those affected by HIV/AIDS (*Nyasa Times*, 2015). A learning group report associated with the Joint Learning Initiative on Children and AIDS at Harvard (Nshakira and Taylor, 2008) revealed that the prevalence of such groups in Uganda was one per 1,300 people.

There are countless local leaders like Saeed around the world who are better placed to reach and walk with marginalized people. Those directly affected have the most vital knowledge, ideas, and resources to deal with the immense and complex problems associated with poverty. People like Saeed see the reality of people's struggles in ways that people with more resources and institutional power cannot.

So we need to ask – what is the cost to *all* of us when so many of the best minds and perspectives from the community level are left out?

Here is where we clearly need all the help we can get. On-the-ground experts welcome.

Summary points

- Deep contextual knowledge is needed for social change.
- Most families get by not because of sweeping national-level policy protections or major internationally-funded programmes but because of local efforts.
- Power, prestige, expertise, and information are concentrated within the do-gooder industry around those with resources. This means that many of the most effective community leaders are outside the conversation.
- Listening to everyday people, who are the experts in their own lives, is vital to the success of any good social endeavour.

About the author

Jennifer Lentfer is director of communications at Thousand Currents (formerly International Development Exchange – IDEX) <https://www.idex.org> in Berkeley, California, although she is based in Washington DC. She was senior writer of aid effectiveness at Oxfam America from 2012 to 2015, and is the creator of the blog how-matters.org <http://www.how-matters.org>.

CHAPTER 6
Respect at the core: Insights on fostering local leadership

Mary Fifield

We squeezed into a two-room cinder block house on a sticky, overcast day in San Pedro de Chimbiyacu to meet with members of 16 families – great-grandmothers, farmers, and young couples from an indigenous Kichwa community in the Ecuadorian Amazon. They had installed household rainwater tanks and planted native trees with a small grant and project management training from Amazon Partnerships Foundation (APF). My colleague Pati and I, representing the APF team, were there to check in and see how the project was going.

The community president welcomed us and turned the meeting over to the inspection team – one man and two women elected from the community who verified how well families were maintaining their tanks.

One of the inspectors reported that 96 per cent of families were keeping their tanks clean, exceeding the target they set for themselves of 85 per cent. Pati and I congratulated them on their outstanding effort. Several other communities with which APF had worked had successfully installed the same rainwater catchment systems and conducted inspections, but no other group had achieved such a high maintenance score.

Marcelina, who wore her long, black hair in a loose ponytail like most of the other women, and whom I'd seen at all the previous meetings, motioned to speak from where she was standing in the back.

'*Compañeros*', she began sombrely. I noticed the dismayed look on her face. 'Thanks to this project, we finally have potable water and we don't have to drink from the streams.' Her eyes were now rimmed in red. Yet even as her voice began to waver, her resolve grew. 'Each and every one of us should have 100 per cent clean tanks all the time because it is our responsibility to make sure our kids are healthy. There is no excuse. Water is life!' she exclaimed.

I was taken aback. In almost a decade of community development work, I had never seen such an emotional and heartfelt plea from one community member to others. Pati, who is Kichwa and has family in rural communities, looked as astonished as I was. A few people mumbled in sheepish agreement and some nodded their heads. Then a hush fell over the room as the gravity of Marcelina's statement sank in.

http://dx.doi.org/10.3362/9781780449302.006

We thanked Marcelina for her powerful words and asked the group how they could get to 100 per cent.

'I don't think Marcelina's ever said two words before today,' I said to Pati afterwards, as we hiked down the gravel road to catch the bus back to the office. 'It was incredible.'

'I know,' Pati agreed, pulling her braid through her backpack strap as she adjusted it on her shoulder. 'They knew she was right. People took what she said seriously.'

Six months later, Marcelina – grandmother, farmer, and craft-maker who had completed some high school but hadn't graduated – was elected president of San Pedro de Chimbiyacu, as the community surpassed most of its own project goals and qualified for another grant from Amazon Partnerships. Under her leadership, the community launched another successful rainwater project (for which they raised half of the budget themselves), expanded the cooperative of women artisans, and turned a community garden into a money-making enterprise.

From empowerment to leadership

Empowerment is fundamentally an individual process: a person recognizes their own power and acts on it. Although outside forces can certainly play an important role, empowerment is an internal transformation. My experience with Marcelina and San Pedro de Chimbiyacu highlighted the difference to me between empowerment and leadership.

Marcelina's empowerment – her personal power and belief in herself – fuelled her impassioned stand for her community to raise its own bar, and certainly her words alone had an influence. But in running for and being elected president, she made a deeper commitment to her community to lead others and foster *their* sense of internal power. Her leadership was driven not just by her individual sense of power, but by her desire, capacity, and vision for expressing her empowerment to help move others toward a shared goal. Becoming a leader was an externally focused process.

This kind of leadership creates change not just for individuals, but for entire communities and regions. A greater sense of personal power is critical and should be an outcome of any development project, but leadership is what leverages that power and catalyzes transformation on a larger scale. To cultivate local leadership, we must be intentional: we have to take cues from the context in which we are working, resist the temptation to rely on cookie-cutter solutions, and recognize that we must be in it for the long haul.

Relationships matter

A group of Ecuadorian and North American colleagues and I created APF in rural eastern Ecuador in early 2009. By providing small grants and project-management training, we supported indigenous communities designing and

---

Box 6.1 Moving day: An aid analogy

By Jennifer Lentfer

What does it feel like to be a citizen on the receiving end of international aid? Here's an analogy to try to help you understand:

Let's say you're moving across town. You have to be out of your old apartment by 5 p.m. that day. You've got the boxes already packed and the moving van rented. All you need is some muscle to help you move the heavy stuff.

You ask your friend to come over early. The plan is to load your bed and couch and dining room table into the truck first, followed by the small stuff. You ask them to come at 9 a.m.

You rise. The day begins, and you busy yourself. There are so many details to take care of when moving. Working industriously, you finally look up at the clock at 10 a.m. There's no sign of your friend.

You text them, 'You on your way?'

You communicate because you know that there's no way you can move that heavy wooden dining room table on your own. At the same time, they are doing you a favour, so you can't appear too annoyed when … they finally show up at 1 p.m.!

In the meantime, you made due. You spent the time loading up just one side of the truck so that when your friend finally arrived, you could hopefully squeeze in the remaining large items.

'Oh hi,' your friend says, unapologetically, as they arrive at your door. 'I'm really sorry, but I can't stay.'

Before you get a chance to register your dismay at their insensitivity to your situation, they say, 'But I brought a hand truck for you to use.'

'Well, at this point, that's not going to be …' you trail off.

There's no point going on. Your 'friend' has already split down the street.

When was the last time you needed help, but had to work on someone else's timeline? When, despite your own plans and efforts, what you need it was assumed?

---

implementing their own projects to confront climate change and promote sustainable development. The APF model was rooted in community self-determination; communities set their priorities and took ownership of the projects from beginning to end.

In a region where the predominant development approach reinforced paternalism and dependency on outsiders, APF's community self-development methodology stood out. If a community expressed interest in applying for a grant, we facilitated workshops to help members brainstorm ideas for projects that would fit their priorities, and then make plans leading to their application to APF. If our board approved their application, the community would receive a grant and intensive training to implement and evaluate their project. Their own results would qualify them for follow-on support. Unlike most aid agencies and organizations, which introduced projects in any and all communities, we worked only with communities that self-identified as the drivers of their projects and wanted to collaborate with us as partners, not as recipients of assistance.

Our board was a team of Kichwa, mestizo, US, and Canadian members that understood the advantages of giving small grants. We set a cap of $2,000 per project, which allowed us to fund a larger number of communities with our modest budget. We were also keenly aware of the distorting effect that large infusions of cash can have on communities without mechanisms to ensure accountability, transparency, and shared benefit. Small grants helped us avoid endangering social cohesion.

APF's relationships with communities were our most important asset and the driver of the methodology. We tended to those relationships in a number of ways. For one, we always waited until we were invited to the community to begin exploring a collaboration, and we held most of our meetings and workshops where people lived, since the communities were sometimes a two- or three-hour bus ride from our office in the provincial capital.

As funders, we recognized the power inherent in our position, but we attempted to flatten that hierarchy as much as possible. Through dialogue with community members, we established clear expectations of each party's responsibilities to the other and to the project at the outset, as evidenced by Marcelina's plea for 100 per cent clean tanks. This intentional communication was necessary because the APF method was so different from what people had experienced with other aid organizations. It was also crucial for building trust and chipping away at paternalism.

Explicitly defining the work as a mutual arrangement between the community and APF helped create an atmosphere of partnership and equality. Each party brought assets to the table: non-tangible ones, like social capital and knowledge, as well as tangible ones, such as money. All communities made a contribution to their project's budget, most often with labour and supplies, and occasionally with cash.

Finally, we reflected on our experience and our relationships at regular intervals. We made reports after every project meeting or workshop and reviewed them at the end of each grant cycle as a board and staff. We applied what we discovered to our process: for example, we learned how to simplify our application process, collect more meaningful baseline data, and look for early signs of a community's level of interest and commitment. Outside evaluators who had an understanding of, and appreciation for, Kichwa communities' culture and experience helped us track what worked, what didn't, and why. Most importantly, many community members gave us direct and frank feedback, and all communities evaluated their results, which helped us learn what was most important to them.

In four years we funded eleven communities whose projects ranged from rainwater catchment systems to organic farming to ecological sanitation. We saw solid evidence of empowerment in each. In communities where women attended meetings but were usually too shy to speak in public, they would give reports in front of the whole group, perform skits during workshops, and volunteer for roles such as committee president, treasurer, or inspector. People who had never had the opportunity to manage their own projects came up with ideas on how to improve the process. They helped design some of the tools and workshop activities that would later form part of APF's *Community Self-Development Methodology Handbook*. Seventy-five percent of communities successfully completed projects through their own design and implementation efforts.

The advocacy gap

Based on the APF's collective understanding of the culture, politics, and history of the region, we expected that the successfully completed projects would have a multiplier effect; that is change that began at the community level would ripple out through the region. As communities became increasingly self-organized and experienced in planning and executing their own projects, they would cultivate or hone the skills to advocate for their agenda with local and regional government officials.

We learned, however, that there was a gap between communities collectively doing work in their most immediate locality and applying that experience to influence policymakers and public attitudes. Families were working together, and their success inspired other communities to work with APF or launch their own projects. But communities weren't necessarily collaborating with others to effect change on a larger or systemic scale.

As the long history of indigenous federations in the region proved, there was certainly a precedent for leaders organizing outside of their communities. However, most federations formed to advocate for indigenous rights and representation primarily at the national level, so there were untapped opportunities to make change locally. Eventually APF realized that if we wanted to help leaders from different communities build coalitions and advocate for their vision of sustainable development with regional officials, we needed different tactics.

Gaining traction with government

After two years of engagement, I convinced two high-level directors from the environment ministry to travel with me to Palma Amazónica, a small rural community down a badly-rutted dirt road and across a river that would swell suddenly in the rainy season. There we met Maria and her husband Venancio, who greeted us in his trademark knee-high rubber boots and button-down shirt. The elderly farming couple had installed a rainwater catchment system, built a composting toilet, and planted some native hardwood and fruit trees through two projects with APF.

After Venancio showed us the toilet, Maria, who was hardly taller than the water tank itself, swiftly unscrewed the two-foot diameter top to show the directors how clean the water was. She explained how much easier it was to have potable water right at the house and a safe place to go to the toilet, though she said she still had to remind her young grandchildren to throw the sawdust (to aid decomposition) in the right place.

The five of us then talked over Maria's toasted *cacao blanco* and *chicha*, a fermented drink that is a cornerstone of Kichwa culture. I could tell that both directors were moved in a way they never were by meetings in their conference room. Later the two of them kicked the soccer ball around with some of the grandkids.

'That was one of the most meaningful things I have done in a long time', one of the directors told me when the three of us rode back to town.

Although the ministry had jurisdiction throughout the province, their top-down programme plan forced their community outreach to be limited by narrow parameters and objectives, so there were many communities where they had no connections. By contrast, our model allowed us to be nimble and form relationships organically, sometimes through people from one community who introduced us to their friends and relatives in another. This meant we could use our position as funder to facilitate connecting real people and ideas to local officials.

Shortly after the visit, the other director told me he was going to submit a proposal to his supervisor for a similar rainwater catchment project with cacao farmers in another province.

The visit was meaningful for us too, because we learned that the ripple effect needed a little nudge. We learned we could connect community leaders to local officials – empowering everyone in the process.

When community members become local officials

The Campana Cocha community had requested that the provincial government provide an expensive, unreliable system of pipes (known as *agua entubada*) to deliver water from streams. The water wasn't potable and there was no environmental impact study to determine how the system would affect the watershed, but this was common practice and the only solution the government offered for communities without water access.

Campana Cocha was one of the first communities with which APF partnered. The project began as a pilot for rainwater systems for drinking water and ecological sanitation. The leaders were interested in it only as a temporary fix until they could get *agua entubada* installed by the government.

Two years later, the community had completed the pilot, followed by a larger project funded partly by APF and led by Angel, an accountant and father of seven who was then the community's vice president. More than 60 families and teachers in five preschools had installed rainwater catchment systems, seven families had built composting toilets, and about half of the participants had planted native hardwoods and fruit trees.

In that time attitudes had also changed dramatically. Now community members were exploring ways to turn Campana Cocha into an 'eco-community'.

Angel, who had recently become community president, invited me to a planning meeting in which Campana Cocha residents were discussing reforesting the community area, which had been cleared to construct dozens of cinder block houses built by a public works agency. They also discussed participating in an eco-tourism project with the environment ministry, and expanding the rainwater catchment project so they could use rainwater for laundry and bathing as well as drinking and cooking. The *agua entubada* project, which had become mired in government bureaucracy, didn't even come up.

Later Angel joined APF's board and then was elected to a seat on the parish council. Shortly after he took office, he authorized rainwater catchment systems for a community of ten families in his jurisdiction.

Angel transformed his personal power into leadership as an elected official, and in that role he could influence other government representatives and advocate for approaches that he knew worked from direct experience in his community.

What fostering local leadership requires

At the end of the day, fostering local leadership means retooling our own systems, our thinking, and our ways of relating to each other so they reflect our commitment to development as a *human* endeavour – one that requires respect, trust, and mutual responsibility.

Coming together with communities under the premise that we were equal parties with a shared interest revealed four important lessons about supporting local leadership development:

1. **Listen closely and embrace uncertainty.** A spirit of respectful inquiry helps organizations avoid making big, irreparable mistakes. Through trial, error, and feedback from communities, we could predict fairly accurately what would work and what wouldn't, but outcomes were never guaranteed. The best hope of succeeding was to continue building relationships out of principle and necessity, familiarizing ourselves with the political and cultural landscape, and coming up with ideas based on our evolving collective knowledge.
2. **Choose thoughtful experimentation over 'tickbox' solutions.** Many ideas that look good on paper (and are widely popular) fail in practice. We had to resist the urge to rely on solutions that made us feel productive, but did not create the change we hoped to see. Collaboration often requires softer approaches for connecting people.
3. **Focus on the long game.** Results often have a long incubation period. Committing to long-term local solutions requires stamina, a healthy preparation for setbacks, and continued funding. Just funding projects that yield numerical outcomes creates a false sense of accomplishment in the short term.
4. **Learning these lessons will help us scale up.** In APF's experience, when people in positions of power listen to community members with good ideas and link them to other communities, the scale of the impact is

increased. This is very different from exponential increases in the number of participants, units produced, regions covered, etc. Projects built on relationships cannot simply be expanded and replicated mechanically, and this applies even more so to leadership development, but the results can be more lasting.

Ultimately, if we want to bring about the change we so desperately need to keep the planet liveable and make it equitable for our children, we need to put relationships of mutual respect at the centre of our work. Real impact comes through conversation, brainstorming, connections to new people, and processes that foster authentic, respectful dialogue and power sharing.

Summary points

- Empowerment is fundamentally an individual process: a person recognizes their own power and acts on it.
- Becoming a leader, or helping move others toward a shared goal, is an externally focused process. Leadership is what leverages that power and catalyzes transformation on a larger scale.
- Projects built on relationships cannot simply be expanded and replicated mechanically. Investing in the conditions through which principled local leaders can ascend and influence the world around them is a better way to scale up.
- Fostering local leadership means reflecting our commitment to development as a *human* endeavour – one that requires respect, trust, and mutual responsibility.

About the author

Mary Fifield is the principal consultant at Kaleidoscope Consulting <http://meetkaleidoscope.com> in Portland, Oregon. She founded Amazon Partnerships Foundation in Ecuador and served as executive director from 2008–2012.

Notes

1. A 501(c) organization is a tax-exempt non-profit organization in the United States. 501 (c)(3) organizations have one of the following purposes: 'religious, educational, charitable, scientific, literary, testing for public safety, to foster national or international amateur sports competition, or prevention of cruelty to children or animals organizations' (IRS, 2008).
2. The Collaborative for Development Action (CDA) 'Listening Project' organized teams of 'listeners' across 20 countries to gather the voices and insights of people active in development. Their report, *Time to Listen* (Anderson et al., 2012) concluded, based on these consultations, that the current 'top-down direction of goods and services violates the principles of participation, ownership, and sustainability essential for effective aid'.
3. Name changed.

References

Anderson, M., Brown, D. and Jean, I. (2012) *Time to Listen: Hearing People on the Receiving End of International Aid*, CDA Collaborative Learning Projects, <http://cdacollaborative.org/publication/time-to-listen-hearing-people-on-the-receiving-end-of-international-aid> [accessed 19 September 2016].

Central Statistical Office (2008) *Swaziland Demographic and Health Survey 2006-07*, Macro International Inc., Available from: <http://dhsprogram.com/pubs/pdf/fr202/fr202.pdf> [accessed 19 September 2016].

Development Initiatives (2014) 'International Aid Transparency Initiative reaches critical mass' in The Development Initiatives [blog] <http://devinit.org/#!/post/international-aid-transparency-initiative-reaches-critical-mass> (posted 7 May 2014) [accessed 19 September 2016].

Engineers without Borders (2016) *Admitting failure* [website] <https://www.ewb.ca/en/about-us/governance/annual-report/> [accessed 19 September 2016].

Fifield, M. (2012) Community Self-Development Methodology: Implementation Handbook, Amazon Partnerships Foundation, <http://www.amazonpartnerships.org/publications/> [accessed 15 February 2017].

'Forum pen Malawi Aids Commission over CBOs funding' (2015) *Nyasa Times*, <http://www.nyasatimes.com/forum-pen-malawi-aids-commission-over-cbos-funding> (posted 2 February 2015) [accessed 19 September 2016].

Global Fund for Children (2013) *A Grassroots Manifesto* [report] <http://www.globalfundforchildren.org/wp-content/uploads/2012/01/Grassroots_manifesto_online.pdf> [accessed 19 September 2016].

Heifer International (2016) *About Heifer International* [website] <http://www.heifer.org/about-heifer/index.html> [accessed 19 September 2016].

IRS (2008) *Publication 557: Tax-Exempt Status For Your Organization (PDF)*. Internal Revenue Service, June 2008. pp. 65–66. <https://www.irs.gov/pub/irs-pdf/p557.pdf> [retrieved 27 January 2009].

Karnofsky, H. (2011) 'Celebrated charities that we don't recommend' in The GiveWell Blog [blog] <http://blog.givewell.org/2009/12/28/celebrated-charities-that-we-dont-recommend> (posted 28 December 2009, updated on 18 August 2011) [accessed 19 September 2016].

Kristof, N. (2010) 'D.I.Y. foreign-aid revolution', *The New York Times*, <http://www.nytimes.com/2010/10/24/magazine/24volunteerism-t.html> (posted 20 October 2010) [accessed 19 September 2016].

Masten, A.S. (2009) 'Ordinary Magic: Lessons from research on resilience in human development', *Education Canada* 49(3): 28–32.

Nshakira, N. and Taylor, N. (2008) *Strengthening mechanisms for channelling resources to child protection and support initiatives: Learning from communities supporting vulnerable children in Uganda*, [report] Joint Learning Initiative on Children and HIV/AIDS, Learning Group 2: Community Action, in collaboration with FARST Africa, Uganda.

Peace Direct (2014) *Local First in practice: Unlocking the power to get things done.* Peace Direct <http://www.peacedirect.org/wp-content/uploads/2015/10/Local-First-In-Action-summary.pdf> (posted 30 October 2014) [accessed 19 September 2016].

UNDP (2010) *Swaziland Household Income and Expenditure Survey 2010* [online]. Available from: <http://www.sz.undp.org/content/swaziland/en/home/library/poverty/shies-2010.html> [accessed 19 September 2016].

PART II

Smart Risk Number 2: Being non-prescriptive and flexible, with a long-term outlook

Non-prescriptive, flexible funding allows local organizations to respond to realities on the ground. Long-term relationships give time and space to address complex problems with long-lasting solutions.

Keywords: capacity building; peer-to-peer learning; innovation; scaling-up; creative solutions

CHAPTER 7

Unearthing community wisdom: Patience, perseverance, and partnerships

Rajiv Khanna

It had been almost 15 years. The people of Chhaperiya village in the Indian state of Rajasthan were still working out how to manage a village-owned common pastureland. It seemed the process of building community unity had much in common with the region's terrain – undulating, rocky, harsh, and cumbersome.

There was a lot at stake for the families in southern Rajasthan's semi-arid climate ecosystem. Agriculture and livestock rearing are the mainstays of the region. But, due to small, fragmented landholdings and drought, farming is highly vulnerable, often only meeting the subsistence needs of families. Animal husbandry is the main source of livelihood, but water is scarce and arable land is very limited. The common pastureland comprised about twenty per cent of the entire village's land and had the potential to supply fuel and fodder needs for the whole community.

Sahyog Sansthan is a non-profit organization that works on natural resource management and sustainable agriculture in rural areas of south Rajasthan. Working with indigenous people and women in particular, it promotes self-help groups and encourages communities to work together to improve their livelihoods. With community support, Sahyog has helped regenerate thousands of acres of degraded land through soil and water management, small-scale irrigation, and sustainable agriculture.

When the villagers first approached the organization 15 years ago, it took an important step: it did nothing. Sahyog knew that the 104 households of indigenous peoples (more than 800 people) in the village would figure it out on their own.

Eventually, the scenario completely changed. By 2013, Chhaperiya's community members:

- were jointly managing 62 hectares (about 153 acres) of land;
- had regenerated 260 native species of trees to maintain the region's natural biodiversity;
- were operating a bank account to track income and expenditure on the pastureland;

http://dx.doi.org/10.3362/9781780449302.007

- were dividing the earnings equally amongst all households; and
- were successfully meeting their fuel and fodder needs.

So, how did the villagers of Chhaperiya start to work together?

The long path to collaboration

Historically, indigenous communities in Rajasthan have faced marginal-ization and exclusion and have lower socio-economic development indicators than non-indigenous populations. The community members first approached Sahyog Sansthan in the early 1990s to request a modest food-for-work programme, in which able-bodied community members exchange labour in public works projects for food.

Around the same time as the food-for-work programme, Sahyog Sansthan also facilitated the formation of a self-help group in Chhaperiya, where 10 to 15 villagers came together to form a savings group. The groups enable people to save money together and then members take small loans from these savings – an alternative for people unlikely to be served by brick-and-mortar financial institutions. Gradually, the villagers used this model as a vehicle for enhanced livelihood options and economic betterment for their families.

Almost a decade after the formation of the self-help group, in 2001, Chhaperiya's residents decided to combine their efforts once again – this time for a drought mitigation and soil conservation programme. Because of the low average rainfall and the unavailability of arable land in the region, the community had prioritized these programmes. The villagers worked together on common pastureland development and, in 2003, the community fenced the perimeter of the pastureland to prevent encroachment and illicit felling. The villagers also decided to share the maintenance costs and the fodder.

Once again, Sahyog did 'nothing' in terms of coming up with outside solutions, but they did accompany the community in their planning, facilitated community dialogue and decision-making processes, and provided technical inputs on land regeneration and biodiversity conservation as requested by the community. Above all, Sahyog served as a trusted friend and advisor to community leaders.

Just as it seemed that the villagers' collaboration was burgeoning, one errant community member decided to encroach on a part of the pastureland to line his own pockets. The other community members banished this person from their village, resulting in a legal case being slapped on the residents of Chhaperiya.

Ultimately, the villagers won in court, and decided to hire two community members to protect the pastureland at a cost of Rupees 500 per month (about US$10). By 2012, the villagers had decided that, in order to save costs, two members per family per day would voluntarily keep watch over their common lands. After several hiccups, and through constant consultation and

Table 7.1 Species diversity, Bootstrap Richness Index (species, density and species richness) and Simpson Diversity Index (tree, shrub, herb and grass species)

Species	Protected site			Unprotected (control) site		
	Density	Richness	Diversity	Density	Richness	Diversity
Trees	952.9 (± 213.3)	19.7	2.88	41.7 (± 30.1)	3.63	3.33
Shrubs	2870.6 (± 1492.0)	13.05	1.85	533.3 (± 352.8)	3.89	6.00
Herbs	0	0	0	43.0 (± 18.3)	4.33	2.36
Grass	69.6 (± 10.8)	16.56	6.88	33.7 (± 23.3)	4.67	2.37

Source: Sansthan, 2009.

experimentation, Chhaperiya's members systematically, and independently, removed the barriers to collaboration. Together, they persisted to protect their common interests.

The continuing need for collaboration

Mr Heera Lal Sharma, the founder of Sahyog Sansthan, takes great pride in narrating this story. He shared it with me as we walked through Chhaperiya's common pastureland in the merciless Rajasthan summer heat of 2013, flanked on either side by community members. He strongly believes that the rural poor must be involved in conserving, managing, and strengthening their natural resources, and he is pleased to see that the people of Chhaperiya have taken ownership of their lands. He says that when communities are organized to preserve their ecology, water security and agricultural output are naturally enhanced. This can result in improved economic conditions, reinforcing their work together. Communities should organize, he insists, to not just maintain arable, but also non-arable land.

This community-driven approach had resulted in a quantitative and qualitative increase in grass production and the renewal of common pasture-lands was being replicated in other villages.

However, both Heera Lal and the villagers of Chhaperiya are well aware that their task is not complete. For example, the governments of Rajasthan and India undertake 'plantation' drives under which they distribute saplings to increase the green cover in the state. These saplings, however, are mostly non-native species and can wreak havoc on the local ecology. Heera Lal is doubly proud of the fact that Chhaperiya's common pastureland has been regenerated naturally, without planting any government-sponsored saplings.

Looking ahead, maintaining the sanctity of community ownership over the land will be crucial as there is a continuing threat of encroachment by powerful individuals. They have also seen private corporations 'leasing' surrounding areas (a refined term for 'land-grabbing') to set up wind farms and for mining. This will continue to test the community resilience of Chhaperiya.

Box 7.1 Spotting community ownership

By Jennifer Lentfer

Many international aid projects, programmes, and social enterprises use the term 'community-based'. For some, this term is merely an indication of location. For others, it signifies that an initiative is truly felt by the community to be something led by and done themselves. If an organization or a project is genuinely community-based, it has much more to do with its relationship to its constituency than its geography.

This latter idea's more accurate description is 'community ownership'. This means that assets are owned and controlled through some representative mechanism that allows a community to influence their operation or use and enjoy the benefits arising. This is vital to social change, as the processes of decision making within local relationships and power dynamics are often the make-or-break factor in any project at the community level. In other words, are the people served or involved invested in the outcomes of a programme? Perhaps most importantly, how can we know?

Those working in cross-cultural contexts often have to make assumptions about various aspects of local dynamics. Oftentimes, whether on a site visit or reading through a stack of proposals, a person can be so concerned with what is happening on the ground that the 'how' can be overlooked or ignored. In some cases, especially early in my career, I did this only to find out later that there was some serious tokenism going on or that the so-called representatives of a community were not sanctioned to speak on people's behalf.

Over time, I learned to identify and test my own assumptions about community ownership. I learned that my gut could tell me quite a lot, but that it could also deceive me. I also learned that the questions I ask myself as an outsider could be useful and important tools to determine if a development initiative is occurring for or with the community, a sometimes subtle but vital distinction.

Questions to help spot community ownership

1. Who participated in the planning of the project or programme? How were/are decisions about priorities made?
2. Do community members recognize themselves as part of the local organization's constituency?
3. Are elements of reciprocity present? To what extent are local resources and/or in-kind contributions being mobilized to support the programme?
4. How does the project/programme build upon the efforts of groups or relationships that pre-date formal funding opportunities?
5. Before a particular project began, how did the community demonstrate stewardship of shared resources or prior accomplishments?
6. Is the story you are presented about 'our problems' adequately balanced with the story of 'our endeavours to change this'?
7. Can community members of various ages, gender, position, etc. articulate a project's goals or effects?
8. Are community leaders clear about what how a strategy or activity is affecting or will affect people's daily lives?
9. What is the quality of interaction between members? Is mutual respect and care demonstrated? Are more than just a few people engaged?
10. To what extent is the project/programme you are working on functioning in collaboration with other neighbouring organizations or government officials?

These questions are by no means exhaustive, nor are they meant to be used as a checklist to ensure all aspects of community ownership are present in a project. Rather, the questions contain subjective ideas that are still dependent on one's definition of community, as well as varying contexts and factors. Taken as a whole, they can help us to not only spot, but also uphold and support, community ownership as a fundamental building block of social change.

In the same way that Sahyog accompanies communities for the long term, Thousand Currents (formerly IDEX) accompanies Sahyog for the long haul. We recognize that the process of social change is volatile and non-linear. Hence, our partnership approach to grantmaking involves providing long-term flexible funding for locally-led initiatives and grassroots organizations and movements in the global South. Thousand Currents also works with its grantee partners to scale their successes by building their capacity and leadership; linking them to broader social change movements at the regional, national, and global levels; and amplifying their voices and victories. Essentially, Thousand Currents' partnership approach inverts the paradigm of how international 'aid' efforts have historically been conducted. We rely on the wisdom and strength of people in the global South to tackle powerlessness and exclusion. Most large-scale development efforts are still, however, initiated and led by people external to the community, with results that are often limited or short-lived. Local initiative ensures a readiness for change and ownership of the change process; it reflects cultural, social, political, geographic, and economic realities; and nuances of understanding that outsiders cannot possess.

What the residents of Chhaperiya can teach funders

My organization Thousand Currents' relationship with Sahyog began in 2004, just as this story was unfolding, and our long-term partnership has continued. In this time, we have learned that funders can see greater impact if they accept that full community participation is a process that takes time. Few people concerned with social change would argue that community participation is an imperative for transformative and sustainable change. But the process of social change and community organizing is non-linear and volatile. The sooner we realize the limitations of our specific, short-term outcomes and metrics-driven mindset, the sooner we allow ourselves and our grantees to realize the vision of social transformation that will create a fairer and more just world.

Summary points

- Accompanying communities in their own decision-making processes is much different than imposing solutions.
- Change at the local level takes time, self-organizing especially. Partnership can reflect long-term approaches.
- Long-term flexible funding models recognize and respond to the reality that the process of social change is volatile and non-linear.

About the author

Rajiv Khanna is director of philanthropic partnerships at Thousand Currents (formerly International Development Exchange – IDEX) <https://www.idex.org> in Berkeley, California.

CHAPTER 8
When local leaders say, 'Thanks, but no thanks'

Scott Fifer

Giving impoverished kids in rural areas – who currently have no schooling – the chance to go to boarding schools a couple hours away. Laying down a concrete floor in a makeshift school where kids currently sit and study on dirt. Bringing in qualified teachers from outside to help improve education in remote villages. Clearly, these are all good ideas. *Seemingly*, all good ideas. So did the community I was working with want funding to execute them?

'*Gracias, pero no*'. Thanks, but no thanks.

As founder and executive director of GO Campaign, which improves the lives of orphans and vulnerable children around the world, I have worked hard to create an international grantmaking organization that prides itself on listening to local leaders on the ground. At the same time, it's our responsibility as grantor and steward of public donations to make sure that the funds support children efficiently, effectively, and economically.

We want to fund *local leaders'* ideas about how to best help children and youth in their community; we don't want to fund *our* ideas. Nonetheless, after having made over 200 grants to nearly 100 local leaders in over 30 countries, I like to think we have a few good ideas once in a while. Moreover, sometimes the people may not know exactly what they want from us and they may seek our suggestions.

So when I was in Guerrero, Mexico in 2012, I was spouting off seemingly terrific ideas on how GO Campaign might help improve upon the deplorable lack of education for children in rural communities there. Each idea I offered was met with resistance from the man to whom I wanted to direct our funds.

Abel Barrera Hernández is a human rights activist in Guerrero. He and his team of lawyers at Tlachinollan Centro de Derechos Humanos de La Montaña risk their lives to champion the rights and dignity of the indigenous people of Mexico – people routinely denied basic human rights by the government.

Seeing the conditions of the education system in these villages, or rather the lack thereof, was a sobering sight. When our hosts pointed to one school in Juquila, I had to ask them to repeat themselves. I wondered if it was,

http://dx.doi.org/10.3362/9781780449302.008

in fact, a school. All I saw was a chicken coop. No desks, no chairs, no books – just dirt surrounded by chicken wire. At least it had a roof, unlike the school down the road that was destroyed by a recent earthquake, though that school hadn't had a teacher since February.

In the village of Nuevo Zaragoza, conditions were only mildly better. A wooden shack with a dirt floor served as the community school. At least students here had desks and chairs. However, there was only one teacher for all 12 grades, so she could only spend a couple hours per day with each class.

Driving the long and unforgiving roads between these rural villages in the mountains and valleys of Guerrero, Abel and I put our heads together. How could GO Campaign best help him help the children in these communities? I heard villagers say they wished the schools had floors instead of dirt. How about we provide funds to build a floor? Labourers from the community could be hired and they could use local materials.

Abel said they would love that, but … it's the duty of the Mexican government to ensure there are proper schools for all of its citizens. By law, the Mexican government is supposed to provide these things – like teachers and decent school facilities. But unfortunately, serving indigenous people is not at the top of many Mexican politicians' lists.

Abel asked me, if the community lets the government off the hook, what kind of message does that send? Then he added, what if the floor gets built but the government comes to inspect it and doesn't like it? Then suddenly that school will not be considered an official school and it could lose any chance it has at getting a teacher. The floor could ultimately make life more difficult instead of helping. Yes, they want the floor, but they don't want it from us.

Okay, so I offered another idea. How about giving scholarships to the kids? Wouldn't the next best alternative be sending them to boarding schools a couple hours down the mountain where they can get a great education, but still be close to home?

Abel let me know that this was another bad idea. Removing the kids from their village, even only for school months and even though not far away, could be detrimental to their native culture. These villages all have their own traditions, and removing them from their family and community cuts against Abel's perspective that the indigenous cultures must be preserved above all. He said that children sent away from home would stop using their vernacular language. I questioned whether the opportunity for a good education outweighed the loss of tribal culture, but Abel held firm. To him, preserving cultural identity was as important as providing good education. Both were necessary, but never one at the expense of the other.

How about finding ways to attract better teachers? This was not an easy task in these beautiful but harsh mountains where there is often no electricity. But together I was sure we could come up with a plan. Again, Abel said, not a good idea. Any teachers from outside would not speak the local language, and teaching in only Spanish would undermine their rich cultural traditions.

Admittedly, part of me wanted to say to Abel, the hell with the cultural traditions! And to hell with the government! These kids need an education. These kids want and need books and desks and chairs and a floor. But that part of me shut up (mostly). Taking smart risks for the GO Campaign means that any idea we fund has to be an idea borne from and supported by community members. So if the community believes in Abel, I believe in Abel.

My years of grantmaking have taught me to know that I have to risk not knowing it all. This means risking my own ego being bruised as I ask for input, and as I let go of preconceived notions. If a respected leader and human rights champion is telling me my well-intentioned ideas don't fly with him, then I gotta figure he knows more than I do.

By the end of our drive, which included being illegally detained on the side of the road by Mexican authorities (for no particular reason, as is the apparent norm in Mexico), Abel and I had indeed found common ground and had come up with a plan. In Neuvo Zaragoza, we would build a nearby 'community centre' with a floor. The kids could go there and have classes in a safe and healthy environment. Meanwhile, the official school could still petition the government to provide the floor it is their duty to provide. We would also try to source some didactic education materials to keep the kids engaged for the greater part of the day when they have no teacher. The same could be done in Juquila with the building that had been destroyed by the earthquake, and the kids would no longer need to study in the chicken coop.

We also came up with the idea of creating a culturally-appropriate human rights course, piloted by Abel's organization, Tlachinollan, to bring into existing schools in the region. Despite our different ideas about books and floors and teachers, Abel and I completely agreed that if the next generation is not raised to understand and demand their basic human rights, there is little hope for the future of indigenous peoples.

By the time I boarded the plane back home, I was happily surprised that together, Tlachinollan and GO Campaign had found a plan of action. On GO Campaign's part, we did it by listening. (And indeed, up to this minute, plans there have continued to change and evolve as the teams continue to assess the needs of the children.)

So the lesson? Don't bring solutions into a community. Rather, come *out* of a community with solutions. It's not about the funding being offered. It's very much about how the ideas are formed and about how the support is delivered. I knew all that before going to Mexico, but it's a lesson I have to learn again and again and a risk I have to be willing to take again and again. It's taught to me differently, in every village, in every country, by every local hero.

It used to worry me, this not knowing. But now I realize it's a constant gift. The day I go into a village and I don't learn this lesson, then I know I should be worried.

Box 8.1 The value of feasting

By Jennifer Lentfer

When Carol arrived at the village in rural Indonesia to begin her anthropological dissertation research, she was shocked at the frequency of 'feasts' that took place. This was not a phenomenon she had come to study, and, frankly, she became a bit annoyed at how she perceived it 'disrupted' village life, and presumably her work. The feasts would involve everyone and much effort and time went into these all-day events.

Over time the true nature and reason for the feasts were revealed as Carol carefully observed what really went on at them. What she had initially viewed, from her Westernized vantage point, as a waste or a distraction changed drastically.

What Carol learned was that feasting functioned as a guise for the sharing of food with families in the village who did not have as much. In essence, the feasts allowed food and other items to be redistributed in a way that not only preserved the dignity of the recipients of assistance, but also included them fully in the social life of the village.

How can giving and receiving be made more personal? Can people be made to feel as if their global neighbours are extending care to them? And why is this important? It's the difference between a hand-up and a hand-out. It's the difference between acknowledging a person's personal struggles and giving them hope, rather than just assigning them a number and lining them up to receive sacks of food. It's the difference in the nourishment offered to the soul.

Summary points

- Outsider ideas of what's needed for progress can differ greatly from local perspectives. For example, building or renovating a school that is supposed to be funded by local officials can let government off the hook and allow them to ignore their responsibilities to constituents.
- Indigenous peoples have special considerations in what they prioritize.
- As grantmakers, sometimes we have to risk a bruised ego to admit that we don't know it all.
- Don't bring solutions into a community. Rather, come out of a community with solutions.

About the author

Scott Fifer is founder and CEO of GO Campaign <https://www.gocampaign. org> in Los Angeles, California, USA.

CHAPTER 9
Local leaders in the driver's seat

Tanya Cothran

When farmers and small shop owners in the village of Manyamula, in northern Malawi, needed to buy fertilizer, or build a shop, or get additional capital to expand their business, they had to travel to the town of Mzimba, 22 km away. Mzimba has several microfinance institutions purporting to help the poor gain access to credit.

However one man, Canaan Gondwe, saw that people were not gaining financial security through the loans. Instead they were losing collateral and paying exorbitant interest rates, even up to 48 per cent for a two-week loan!

Gondwe emailed me wanting to find more information about creating a savings and loans group in Manyamula. As a partner of my organization, Spirit in Action International (SIA), Gondwe knew I would be interested in working with him to find an alternative for his village. We have a broad focus for our grants, responding to the needs of the community, which means that I am constantly learning about the various needs of individual communities and the different approaches community groups take to address these needs.

With my librarian-trained research skills, I found some sample documents for village savings and loans groups and a model constitution put together by Trickle Up for their Savings and Credit Groups, and sent them off to Gondwe for him to review and adapt. Canaan and I corresponded for months about ways to organize, get more people involved, and fund this programme.

At the end of 2009, Gondwe gathered together 41 people to form the Manyamula Village Savings and Loans group (MAVISALO). They applied for and received a small grant from SIA to start a poultry house that would serve as the start-up capital for their loan fund, which would enable its members to have access to credit without travelling to Mzimba and paying exploitative interest rates.

Members bought starting shares of about $6.50 each to join the group. Several widows who could not pay the initial fee were invited to participate anyway, with their part funded by the chicken profits.

Since their start in 2010, MAVISALO has grown to 180 members and has a base capital of just over $12,000, which includes member savings and income from interest, and profits from their cooperative poultry and maize-milling businesses.

http://dx.doi.org/10.3362/9781780449302.009

Box 9.1 Why organizations matter[1]

By The Barefoot Collective

Organizations matter. They make it possible for us to pool the strengths we have as individual human beings to achieve things that we could not do alone. They enable us to collectively mobilize our individual powers to face our human challenges with greater possibility.

When ordinary people are able to create, link, and strengthen their own organizations, and through them to voice and act out what they think, feel, and want, they acquire more power over the choices and decisions that affect their lives. For people living in poverty and without basic rights, organization makes a different future possible. In building organizations, one shapes the world.

For example: A group of rural women were assisted by a development agency to start a vegetable garden in their community. The primary intention of the project was to improve the diets of community members. But its ultimate achievements went much further than this. In fact the women learnt so much and took so much courage from being part of the group that their ambitions grew as fruitfully as their seedlings. Before long, they were producing more than their families could eat and selling the surplus. Respectfully presenting themselves to the chief, they petitioned for, and got, more land. Then they yanked a bunch of men off their butts and paid them to fence their new land and build a shed for their tools. It didn't take long before their position in the community had changed as well. They had become a force to contend with. The women began involving others in their work and the project began to include widely divergent aspects of community life, both economic and political. In the end it was the success of their organization rather than the vegetable garden itself that made the greatest impact on the community.

Local organizations begin small, often becoming more than originally intended, like the organization of the women gardeners above. Support from the outside, from funders, non-governmental organizations, activists, or government workers can help, but the will of people to develop does not need to be imported, only unblocked and supported.

The fact that people, under the direst of circumstances, are able to pull themselves together and organize themselves is a celebration of the fact that the impulse to develop and organize is inborn.

MAVISALO's loan repayment rate is 98.8 per cent. Also, because the programme is community-based, the interest generated from the loans (at the rate of 5 per cent per month) goes back into the loan fund so that more people have the opportunity to borrow and expand their businesses.

'Members of MAVISALO are able to save through shares given to this locally-based institution [which they created] and also they are able to access loans for their economic empowerment,' explains Gondwe.

When I visited Manyamula in 2014, I saw that MAVISALO was about more than just loans and economic empowerment. The whole group meets once a month to review their constitution and address any concerns. At these meetings, they work entirely through a consensus agreement so that everyone is included in the discussion. Also, since they work together in the poultry and maize-milling centres, they are building a strong team where everyone contributes.

I came away from my visit so in awe of the local leadership of the project. Canaan Gondwe and the other leaders were able to make this savings and loans group successful by adapting it to fit local realities. And this adaptation is especially important as the programme continues to expand and to face challenges. As the group grew, they divided the membership into geographically oriented teams, so that people can meet in their smaller groups between the monthly meetings. Each of these districts has a leader from the area, which creates a broader leadership base and a more democratic system.

When Gondwe first emailed me, I was keenly aware that, as an outsider, I did not know what worked best for savings and loans in Manyamula Village. Still now I am only beginning to grasp the culture and the context of the work.

But SIA did not have to know all the answers before investing in this project. We took a risk on Canaan Gondwe, his idea, and the rest of the MAVISALO leadership. We have also built a working partnership, listening to and trusting local leadership at the centre, that goes way beyond what SIA or MAVISALO could ever do on its own.

Gondwe was always in the driver's seat. I was lucky to have been invited along for the ride.

Summary points

- Ideas that originate from the ground have a better chance of succeeding. The role of outsiders is to support them.
- Micro-lending institutions are not magic bullets for development. Though the potential to increase income is high, interest rates can also be especially high for rural populations and the poor.
- People have an innate desire to organize themselves. From small ideas, large impact and reach can emerge. Western-based organizations can help local groups find resources and make connections.

About the author

Tanya Cothran is executive administrator of Spirit in Action International <http://spiritinaction.org> in California. She lives in Toronto, Canada.

CHAPTER 10
Leaving the room

Jennifer Lentfer

I greeted everyone warmly as they entered the airy, bright classroom. One by one, representatives from the 24 child-focused community-based organizations arrived to our meeting in Lilongwe. They were excited to meet me, the 'Jennifer' who for many only existed as an email address.

At the time I was the manager of the foundation's Malawi portfolio and I had been responsible for almost doubling the number of grantees. They ranged from more nationally focused child advocacy organizations to emerging groups of citizens organized around their concern for kids, but with few financial resources. The foundation I was working with at the time was providing small grants to the organizations, but I saw a tremendous opportunity for these groups to learn from and lean on each other. Due to the expense, bringing the organizations together was rare, but it was a tremendous opportunity to see what could be done together to strengthen their programmes and advocacy on behalf of children in Malawi.

I knew that I had about $15,000 to spend on capacity building or organizational strengthening for the portfolio. Splitting it among all the grantees equally would leave them each without much. Preferencing the nascent groups, who needed the most support, would also leave the more established groups with their needs unmet.

But I had a plan.

The first day of the meeting was filled with introductions and getting to know each other better as leaders and as organizations. I described our foundation's grantmaking process in depth and answered questions about our funding practices. The grantees shared their work, and their challenges. After a full day, the scene was set.

When day two of our meeting began, I welcomed everyone and then started the day by describing my dilemma about the capacity building funds. Then my plan, or should I say, non-plan, took hold. I told the leaders gathered there, all accomplished and tenacious in their own right, to make a plan for how they would spend the money. I let everyone know exactly how much money our foundation could contribute to this effort. I told them there were no restrictions on how they could spend the money, as long as it would benefit the organizations gathered there in a fair way. Then I told them that I was leaving and would return at the end of the day.

http://dx.doi.org/10.3362/9781780449302.010

People looked confused at first. Leaving? 'Yes, I am leaving,' I confirmed. 'Tea and lunch will be served. You have the classroom. Tell me what you'd like to do as a group.'

'This is a room of leaders who can determine how best to utilize the time, get everyone's ideas and input, and make sound decisions,' I explained. 'I will join you later only to learn what you've discussed, your recommendations for how the funds are spent, and planned steps going forward.' I asked if there were any questions, and then I left the campus.

It was risky, perhaps, to put this responsibility on our grantees' shoulders. But from my previous experience in international aid, I had seen countless capacity building activities, trainings, consultants, seminars, etc., go to waste. The teaching methodologies and the imposition of 'best practices' were often ill-suited to the problems faced by grassroots organizations. I was a big fan of exchange visits and mentoring between organizations, which can offer the most relevant and supportive assistance through sharing on-the-ground experiences.

My philosophy was that, for capacity building to be effective, it must be self-determined. In other words, what people most want to learn or improve is what will get the needed attention and resources. Think about it this way. Your mom says, 'You should really learn to cook.' What if you know you just don't enjoy cooking? What if it makes more sense to you to pick up take-out meals on your way home? This means that probably, you won't ever invest the time to learn to cook. But if cooking is something that interests you, and you've been wanting to win over a new love interest with a romantic meal, then you might be more inclined.

When I returned to the grantees' classroom at the end of the day, I was blown away. Not only was there a strategy for how the money would be used through a series of peer-to-peer learning opportunities among the grantees, there was an extensive plan with set goals, distributed responsibilities, and a concrete timeline. The budget was for more than the amount I could offer, but they assured me, with confidence, that this initiative could be of interest to other donors and that our $15,000 would get them started on the right track.

Before the end of the year, the group faced some growing pains. In one email exchange, a leader challenged the 'hierarchy' that was assumed between the more established organizations in the larger cities and the smaller groups in the rural areas. Eventually, both parties agreed that they had much to learn from each other.

Less than a year later, I moved on to a different position in the foundation and handed the Malawi portfolio over, but initial activities were up and running. Eventually I left the foundation. But small grants based on trust mean that relationships don't end. It was five years later when a colleague still at the foundation gave me a call. She was excited to share with me the progress of the network that had been formed that day.

'You should see the network in the north today, Jen! You wouldn't believe how they're helping each other.' The partner network was now a key part of the foundation's work in Malawi, but, more importantly, it had been wholly taken up by the grantees. 'All I could think about when I was hearing the update today,' she said, 'was how you had the courage to hand over that partner meeting, so many years ago'.

Setting up a strong grantee network that day had not been my intent. I simply looked to this group of devoted and driven community leaders to come to my aid, to tell me how they wanted to come together and share skills and resources.

Sometimes, the most effective partnership strategy might just be to get out of the way.

Summary points

- For capacity-building to be effective, it must be self-determined.
- The teaching methodologies and the imposition of best practices are often ill-suited to the problems faced by organizations on the ground.
- External influence warps dialogue. Giving time for brainstorming solutions, without outsiders in the room, can produce fruitful, creative solutions.
- What feels 'risky' (even to grantees) may unleash the most potential.

About the author

Jennifer Lentfer is director of communications at Thousand Currents (Formerly International Development Exchange – IDEX) <https://www.idex. org> in Berkeley, California, although she is based in Washington DC. She was senior writer of aid effectiveness at Oxfam America from 2012 to 2015, and is the creator of the blog how-matters.org <http://www.how-matters.org>.

CHAPTER 11

When small is too small: Recognizing opportunities to scale smart risks

Caitlin Stanton

The phrase 'small grants, big impact' was printed on the back of all of our business cards for several years at the Global Fund for Women. Eventually, we grew less comfortable with this tagline.

During the time I was part of the foundation, over a decade, the Global Fund for Women collectively awarded more than $80 million in small grants, the vast majority of them less than $20,000 in size. Working on evaluation, I saw the evidence for small grants as smart risks first hand.

There was a $4,000 seed grant awarded to group of women in Yunnan Province who used it to launch an organization that went on to reduce the use of carcinogenic pesticides in rice production in China. Or the seed grants awarded in the 1990s for a handful of underground schools in Afghanistan that grew into the Afghan Institute for Learning, which today provides health services and education to over 300,000 people annually.

Feminist movements, funded for many years solely by small donations and grants, are responsible for enormously significant changes in policies and laws on domestic violence (Htun and Weldon, 2012) - changes that have codified a legal right to live free from violence in the home for well over one billion women and girls globally.

In the United States, small grants played an important role in launching the LGBTQ rights movement, awarded by donors like the Horizons Foundation and the Astraea Lesbian Foundation for Justice. Speaking about what was at that time an emerging movement, Howard Brown, co-founder of the National Gay and Lesbian Task Force, said in 1973 'we're a bargain for a foundation ... They could make a big contribution to civil rights for very little money' (Bowen, 2012).

More recently, small grants have supported emerging LGBTQ movements globally. These grants, like one awarded by the Urgent Action Fund grant for a groundbreaking Pride parade in Hanoi, Vietnam, or the support given by social-justice funders to LGBTQ groups in Uganda and Kenya, challenge unjust laws and uplift values of human dignity, love, and equality.

Routinely, I find myself awed by the extent of the progress achieved through the investment of comparatively small amounts of funding

http://dx.doi.org/10.3362/9781780449302.011

when that funding is provided with respect, trust, and flexibility to those directly engaged in the struggle for change. So why would I become uncomfortable with the 'small grants, big impact' tagline?

Smaller is not always smart

I began to see the limitations of small grants, and the opportunities for bigger ones, in the reports on their activities that groups would submit to the Global Fund for Women. One group wrote about having to make the choice to keep the heat off in their office in the winter to save funds. Another could have implemented a brilliant programme for girls far more widely had they had additional funding. Many relied heavily on volunteers and could not afford to pay staff.

Community groups and donors alike need to recognize the need and opportunities for big grants, in addition to small grants, when invested in grassroots groups at the local level. At some point between starting a community-based organization to address domestic violence and getting national legislative change, the investment needs to scale alongside the potential for impact.

I think about the dynamic women's group in the Philippines working on land rights and climate change that wrote, as did too many others, 'we have no paid staff, because we cannot afford to have paid staff.' I think about all the times I met a group doing good work with a $15,000 grant and wondered what they might have been able to do with $30,000.

The systemic underfunding of some of the key mechanisms for sustainability (fundraising systems, leadership development) by donors to US non-profits is well-documented (Bell and Cornelius, 2013). This situation may be exponentially worse for non-profits in the global South. I think about how the median operating budget for the women's rights organizations in the database at the Global Fund for Women hovered for years around just $35,000.

At the end of the day, what I see most of all is untapped potential.

Who is not 'playing big'?

The truth is that societies do a pretty good job of telling people on the margins of society that smaller is better. Too often, women and girls already play small instead of playing big. We know that women are less likely to ask for salary increases or promotions than men (Ludden, 2011), and that women are less likely to write op-eds or give 'expert' commentary than men (Yaeger, 2012).

Simply put, women are already prone to downplay their ideas and to ask for smaller amounts of money. When HelpAge International, a UK-based network that makes small grants to help elders improve their lives, asked a group of women and a group of men to come up with proposals for improving livelihoods in their village in Kenya, the men asked for 67 per cent more funding than the women (Collodel, 2011).

I no longer felt comfortable with the 'small grants, big impact' tagline because I got tired of reading about downsized plans. I got tired of seeing

---

Box 11.1 Go deep or go wide?

By Jennifer Lentfer

'But how can we take it to scale?'

'Scaling up' is often on the minds of those in the social-good sector. We have to reach more people, show more impact (and now!) after all, don't we?

Scaling up is most usually associated with increasing the size, amount, or importance of something. And it often focuses people on ploughing ahead, rather than allowing for failure, iterative learning, and adjustment.

Consider a cost and cost-benefit analysis to help frame the issues at hand:

If one project reaches 100 girls at a cost of $1.00 per girl, while a second project reaches 1,000 girls at the cost of $1.10 per child, funders might be tempted to declare the first project more 'efficient'. However, such a decision would prioritize 'efficiency' over coverage, and 900 fewer girls would be reached. Funders must decide then if the opportunity costs of reaching more girls are greater than the extra $0.10 per girl.

On the other hand, funders must also consider whether to prioritize coverage over quality. Perhaps the project serving 100 girls is very intensive and long term, for example reaching and rehabilitating girls that have been part of the sex trade, while the project serving 1,000 girls provides a single workshop on reproductive and sexual health. Fundamentally changing the lives of a few girls might have a more significant long-term impact than helping many more girls with a more 'shallow' or one-off activity.

To effectively support grassroots efforts, we may need a new definition of scaling-up. For example, community-based organizations, often under-resourced, have no choice but to build close ties with other key stakeholders to achieve their mission and help access services for people. What if scaling-up meant being deeply networked with peer organizations, and local government, and private sector entities? What if scaling-up meant influencing change at higher policy- or decision-making levels? What if scaling-up meant collaborative efforts demonstrating shared, collective impact?

More thoughtful discussions of scaling-up might make more room for local solutions, community leadership, and grassroots movements and organizations to take part. What if instead of rushing and pushing to go wide, we could allow things to play out in their own time, and go deeper?

---

ambitious and innovative strategies sacrificed in favour of what was safer and easier to fit in the budget for a small grant.

Smart risks need transformative resources

When locally-led groups see an opportunity to play big, we should think strategically about how to resource that opportunity. We are ready to move beyond capping grant sizes at very low levels or only utilizing very small grants. Over the past five years, some women's funds have increased their grant size and now also make grants at levels of $50,000 and up. However, many grassroots movements remain sorely and consistently underfunded. They are ready for more.

To be clear, I'm not arguing that growth is always good or that big is always better. There remains a role for $5,000 grants. Small grants can still upend traditional philanthropy and catalyze social change. And large grants going to grassroots organizations or movements that are not ready to manage them can be overwhelming, so appropriateness is key. But human-rights and social-justice movements begun in the last century are maturing. Organizations, even locally led grassroots organizations, can identify opportunities where $20,000 and $50,000 and $100,000 grants would be more strategic.

Thinking more about how we can increase funding also means thinking more about how we collaborate. Sometimes a $10,000 grant becomes $30,000, not because one donor changes their level of funding, but because they found others who could co-fund with them. This forces funders to talk to each other more, plan together more, learn together more. Where our own resources seem small, our collective resources are more powerful. Rita Thapa, the founder of Tewa, the Nepal Women's Fund, once said of the small grants that Tewa awards to community groups:

> It makes a difference, you know, to receive a grant that is not from a government or a big foundation, but that we know was cobbled together from many small gifts contributed by other women. Groups treat this kind of money more carefully.

Small grants have played a powerful role in seeding human-rights and social-justice movements at the grassroots. Taking smart risks means not underestimating the enormous quantities of 'people power' and the unquantifiable vision, outrage, and guts that are perhaps the most important part of social transformation.

There are times when small is too small. Where communities have historically been under-resourced, it is important and strategic to guard against over-romanticizing small grants and sacrificing impact. In these cases, we must speak up and be both funders and advocates for a transformative level of resources. While we celebrate small grants as smart risks, we must also challenge ourselves to recognize big ideas that may emerge from the grassroots with the potential for scale.

Summary points

- Small grants have fuelled important social movements.
- Failing to recognize moments when a larger grant is needed is leaving potential untapped.
- Local groups can do more with more. When locally led groups see an opportunity to play big, we should think strategically about how to resource that opportunity.

About the author

Caitlin Stanton is director of learning and partnerships at Urgent Action Fund <https://urgentactionfund.org> in California, USA. She was senior officer for learning, monitoring and evaluation at the Global Fund for Women from 2001–2013.

Note

1. This essay was originally published in *The Barefoot Guide to Working with Organizations and Social Change*, by The Barefoot Collective, 2009 Community Development Resource Association: Cape Town, South Africa. Used with permission.

References

Bell, J. and Cornelius, M. (2013) *UnderDeveloped: A National Study of Challenges Facing Nonprofit Fundraising*, CompassPoint Nonprofit Services and the Evelyn and Walter Haas, Jr. Fund, Available from <https://www.compasspoint.org/sites/default/files/documents/UnderDeveloped_CompassPoint_HaasJrFund_January%202013.pdf> [accessed 27 September 2016]

Bowen, A. (2012) *Forty Years of LGBTQ Philanthropy*, Funders for LGBTQ Issues, Available from <http://www.lgbtfunders.org/files/40years_lgbtqphilanthrophy.pdf> [accessed 27 September 2016]

Collodel, A. (2011) *Livelihood grants: Does size matter?*, HelpAge Blogs [blog] <http://www.helpage.org/blogs/andrew-collodel-1769/livelihoods-grants-does-size-matter-380/> (posted 2 December 2011) [accessed 27 September 2016]

Htun, M. and Weldon, S. (2012). The Civic Origins of Progressive Policy Change: Combating Violence against Women in Global Perspective, 1975–2005. *American Political Science Review* 106: 548–569.

Ludden, J. (2011) *Ask For A Raise? Most Women Hesitate*, NPR [website] <http://www.npr.org/2011/02/14/133599768/ask-for-a-raise-most-women-hesitate> (posted 8 February 2011) [accessed 27 September 2016]

Sansthan, S. (2009) *Drought Mitigation Project - Impact Assessment, A Study of Chhaperiya Village in Lasadiya Tehsil*, unpublished.

Yaeger, T. (2012) *Who Narrates The World?*, The OpEd Project [website] <http://www.theopedproject.org/index.php?option=com_content&view=article&id=817&Itemid=103> [accessed 29 September 2016]

PART III

Smart Risk Number 3: Looking to the grassroots for innovation

The most innovative solutions to intractable problems come from local context, priorities, and realities. Innovation is most often a result of failure and when funders can tolerate more risk, local leaders have room to learn and grow.

Keywords: grantmaking; pay it forward; accountability; innovation; entrepreneurs

CHAPTER 12

Small grants as seed funding for entrepreneurs

Caroline J. Mailloux

Global health, workforce, education. Probably you're thinking about scholarships and training for medical, nursing, and pharmacy students. But what about mattresses? Getting people to serve in hospitals and clinics in rural areas in poor countries is difficult, as it is everywhere. But what if mattresses could help solve the problem?

When I worked in a global health non-profit organization, I administered a small grants programme that supported 'innovations' in health workforce education. The idea was simple: students or faculty from training institutions would apply to us to fund short-term projects. The criteria of the small grants were the following: 1) faculty and students from the training institutions must collaborate; 2) the project must fill an education and training gap in the existing curriculum; and 3) the project serve a rural area. The applications that we received astounded us year after year.

Had we set strict criteria on the grant, we never would have learned that one of the major barriers for students to serveing in rural areas was the lack of a clean, safe place to sleep and study. Because many medical and health students in the global South come from wealthier families, we learned that mattresses and the renovation of a simple dormitory in rural Uganda was all that was needed to ensure the students were better positioned to address the medical needs of the communities they were serving. A small grant for mattresses, as prioritized by the students themselves, leveraged university teaching and financial resources, bringing many students to rural areas for the first time to serve and gain hands-on learning. The grant also reinforced a mutual investment between rural communities and students from the health professions, thereby increasing access to care in rural areas. With only a small investment in mattresses, we heard feedback that more students were serving in rural areas after graduation.

Would you consider mattresses innovative?

Local knowledge and contextual expertise are among the most powerful sources for new ideas, concepts, and strategies that meet social needs. This expertise about what communities need and what resources they already possess drives

http://dx.doi.org/10.3362/9781780449302.012

sustainable and collaborative solutions, which, in the case in Uganda, was also a fairly simple one.

Often, what is considered 'innovative' in global development is what's new – the latest idea or product as in the private sector. But what if innovative simply meant including previously excluded people in decision-making and accountability mechanisms? What if innovation were found in the individual and collective reflection processes that people use to identify and overcome obstacles, resulting in changes or adaptations in people's work on the ground? Aren't the people who intimately know a problem from the inside more likely to see where the possibilities for innovation lie? Ultimately, where we are looking for innovation and who defines innovation are most important.

What makes mattresses a smart risk?

Modest funding to support local leaders is functionally similar to seed funding for social entrepreneurs. A drive or entrepreneurial spirit is present in both, as is leveraging social and professional networks. Also present is the under-standing that some investments will thrive, be brought to scale, and positively change the landscape. On the flipside, some initiatives will fizzle, though not necessarily without the benefit of increasing the capacity of grassroots leadership through failure and learning. Local leaders are constantly eliminating iterations of solutions as part of the natural problem-solving process and they reinvest this learning in the community.

Small grants are designed to be put directly into the hands of trusted local experts without getting trapped in the budget lines of huge grants and hindered by the administrative burden of excessive reporting and evaluation. Fundamental to this model is a value shared between the granter and grantee: that community members know best how and where to invest funding to maximize impact. Like seed funding for social entrepreneurs, small grants have repeatedly demonstrated their ability to strengthen human and social capital in unanticipated, synergistic, and systematic ways.

In addition to being more flexible and accessible, small grants promote scalability, local ownership, and community collaboration. Small grants and microgrants can encourage curiosity and a culture of play, which has been proven as crucial to innovation in the business and social enterprise sectors.

Listening and learning for innovation at the grassroots

Many community development and global development practitioners don't think of themselves or community partners as innovators, but small grants can support the development and refinement of new strategies, concepts, and ideas to address complex social issues.

Not all small grant-funded projects will be scaled up or replicated to reach a wider geography or population. That is okay. They can still spark a web of capacity building through leadership development, creative community collaborations, and increased communication between community members and supporting organizations about a community's prioritized needs and solutions. In the scope of action by smaller grassroots groups focused on family and community structures, is there not the potential to draw upon their innovations for larger programmes?

Summary points

- Small grants for local leaders are like seed money for entrepreneurs.
- Among the most powerful sources for new ideas, concepts, and strategies that meet social needs are local knowledge and contextual expertise.
- Who defines innovation matters. We can think of innovation as simply including previously-excluded people in decision-making and accountability mechanisms.

About the author

Caroline J. Mailloux is principal at Caroline J. Mailloux Consulting in Rhode Island, USA.

CHAPTER 13
Grants, not loans

Tanya Cothran

As we have been writing this book, and sharing that we're in the process of doing so at family gatherings, or cocktail parties, or yoga classes, this is the conversation that often ensues:

'Oh you're writing a book! What about?'

With people who don't work in philanthropy, or international aid, or the non-profit sector, I often find myself using a shorthand: 'The book is about the power of small grants.'

What I really mean is the power of flexible and responsive (not necessarily small, but often modest) grants in support of grassroots groups and movements in the global South. 'Cool, small grants,' the person usually exclaims. 'So like microcredit.'

'Actually, no.'

The shadow side of microcredit

In the first decade of the twenty-first century, the Grameen Bank and Kiva became a part of the zeitgeist of 'doing good' overseas. Providing microfinance to individuals in poor countries was lauded as a sustainable, impactful solution – finally – and the idea took hold among the general public. There was a rush to start new microcredit programmes and organizations to benevolently provide pathways out of poverty.

It was thought to be common sense that microloans would ensure the sustainability of anti-poverty programmes because the act of paying back the loan would instil the sense of 'ownership' among the people receiving loans. Therefore, these were considered preferable to microgrants, which were often labelled 'handouts'. The parallels to debates over welfare payments or 'being on the dole' in the US or the UK were apparent. How could microgrants to individuals or families do anything but create a sense of entitlement on the part of those on the receiving end? Though my own organization, Spirit in Action International, gave grants, there were a few vocal board members who thought that switching to loans to the poor in the global South would promote long-term, individual responsibility, as well as help sustain our organization financially.

Unfortunately, we learned that those loan funds can come at a great cost to people in bottom income brackets. Interest rates of 40 to 100 per cent

http://dx.doi.org/10.3362/9781780449302.013

of the loan principal and travel costs to get to and from a bank mean that many people are stuck from the moment they receive the money. In some markets, loans wreak havoc with indebtedness, hostile payment collectors, and inflexible repayment schedules (Rosenberg, 2011; Schicks, 2011). Looking again, could grants more effectively offer financial independence and cultivate small businesses in a community?

Why grants?

A loan is a financial tool used by banks to make money for their shareholders, but Spirit in Action believes that a grant creates space for positive relationships and an empowered individual. Through our Small Business Fund, we provide US$150 microgrants to groups of three to five people, usually family members, in parts of Africa. This money could be used by the group for any business endeavour, usually a microenterprise such as a grocery, bakery, piggery, or craft shop, or as an investment in their farm. If these were loans, we would have to employ a debt collector. Instead, we have local coordinators who train grant recipients in business planning, marketing, and basic accounting before they receive their grant. The grant cohort, usually five business groups, or about 15–20 people, also forms a support group, strengthening communal and social bonds.

Receiving a $150 grant – rather than a loan – means that the first $150 in profit from their successful enterprise can help group members go to school, improve their house, or pay for medical care. Most importantly, the profit is not used to pay back foreign donors. Eventually our pay-it-forward programme, Sharing the Gift, requires that some of the profits down the line are gifted to others in the community, generating goodwill and further progress at the local level.

What's good for the goose ...

Our model of microgrant giving also reflects our home-office organizational practices. Spirit in Action's income relies purely on grants, not loans. We are also grant recipients. Our individual donors don't ask us to pay them back. They ask us to pay their gifts forward to help people as defined in our mission and programmatic plans.

By asking our Small Business Fund grant recipients to pay it forward to a neighbour or community member, rather than paying us back, we are asking them to do only what we ourselves do. Paying it forward starts with our donors and passes on to many more throughout the world.

Creating givers

Our Sharing the Gift programme asks our Small Business Fund grant recipients, 'How can you share this gift with others?' The actual form of sharing varies among groups, with input from the local coordinators. Some tithe a percentage of profits toward future groups, others contribute seeds or baby animals to a new group, and sometimes business groups come together to support a project that benefits the whole community.

People not only become small-business owners after receiving a grant from Spirit in Action International, they become givers, or philanthropists, in their communities (Nikolau, 2016). Any good non-profit fundraiser will tell you that people experience genuine happiness from giving to others (Zaki, 2015). We have seen the personal and community transformation that occurs when people who have grown up with very little to have more to share with others, and become respected for their gifts to neighbours.

Unlike loans, which create an immediate indebtedness in the community, grants and a paying-it-forward mentality make lasting changes in the communities where we have funded small businesses. Even without additional grants, local growth comes from small-business owners themselves. The development of their community originates with their desire to pay forward what they have received and invest in their communities (Cotton, 2011).

These grants are far from a handout.

Summary points

- Microcredit has not proven to radically improve the systems and power structures that keep people in poverty.
- Grants, rather than loans, for entrepreneurial activities can mean that business profits stay with the business owner, rather than being paid back to a Western donor.
- A pay-it-forward programme means that prosperity is shared, and that goodwill and social cohesion are generated at the local level.

About the author

Tanya Cothran is executive administrator of Spirit in Action International <http://spiritinaction.org> in California, USA. She lives in Toronto, Canada.

CHAPTER 14

Building accountability
from the ground up in Liberia[1]

Blair Glencorse

What if there was a way to continually sort through and make meaning of the vast amount of local news, national and international media, so that you could always get the best and most relevant content even without an internet connection?

What if this highly-valued, curated information-sharing platform was in the middle of your town or city? Near one of the busiest intersections? What if it was written not on a screen, but on a blackboard?

If you live in Monrovia, Liberia, it is. *The Daily Talk* is a convenient way that 5,000 people consume their news daily – more people than those that read Liberia's most popular website. Alfred Jomo Sirleaf has been at the forefront of this effort to make sure people have crucial information. Since he founded *The Daily Talk* in 2000, the 42-year-old father of three, inventor, and high-school graduate has been on a personal mission to provide free news on local, national, and international issues to his fellow Liberians.

On Tubman Boulevard, at one of Liberia's capital's busiest thoroughfares, stands a white plywood shack. Every morning, with just four other staff and very little and inconsistent funding, Sirleaf checks in via text with his 'eyes and ears' correspondents across Liberia. They scour newspapers, radio reports, international media, and government websites. Sirleaf then decides which three to four stories and headlines will appear on the shack's 'front page', and writes them up with weatherproof chalk in the small, dark newsroom behind the rotating blackboard.

Sirleaf writes in Liberian English, a vernacular that is readily under-standable to people, and tapes up photos he has printed out in the nearby internet café to illustrate stories. He has also devised a system of symbols that enables people who don't read well to understand the themes of the day's main story.

People can see the bottle of dirty water hung by the shack and know that oil prices are in the news. If it's a blue helmet, readers know it's the UN peace-keepers. For stories about embezzlement (or 'eating money' in the colloquial), it's a broom to signify cleaning house. A metal hubcap signifies a story about the 'iron lady' of Liberian politics, Liberia's Nobel Prize winning president Ellen Sirleaf Johnson (no close relation to *The Daily Talk* founder), who passes

http://dx.doi.org/10.3362/9781780449302.014

by the shack every day in transit from her home to her office at Liberia's Ministry of Foreign Affairs.

Those who can read often do it aloud for their friends that can't and these props or symbols enable people walking by to have conversations with those gathered at the shack, thereby breaking down barriers for people of all ages, classes, and education levels to engage with the issues of the day.

'Without paying a dime, all you need to do is go closer and somebody can help you understand what is happening,' Sirleaf explains. 'I love *The Daily Talk* because it is for the commoners,' Carlos Joseph, a law-enforcement officer told the Voice of America (2010). 'Those who don't have money to buy a newspaper, can read'. Abakou Sammy, an electronics worker also points out, 'You know he [Sirleaf] breaks it down for us, you know, so we understand it better.'

The ability to reach people in ways most relevant to them became even more crucial when Ebola hit Liberia in 2014. 'I started in April. I was covering Ebola when it was still at the border, near Guinea,' says Sirleaf. 'I was scoring the government on its health care facilities, response to the epidemic, communications to the public, lack of preventative systems, etc. *The Daily Talk* is about keeping everyone in the system on their toes and aware of what is happening,' he says.

Sirleaf feels that it was misinformation that created turmoil in Liberia's past, and allowed those with power to manipulate and control people. Before Ebola hit, *New York Times* journalist Lydia Polgreen (2006) wrote that Sirleaf was, 'an information evangelist, fervent in his belief that a well-informed citizenry is the key to the rebirth of his homeland, ravaged by 14 years of civil war'.

Sirleaf's work – before, during, and after Ebola – aims to fuel active citizenship so that people are able to turn to politics and debate, rather than armed conflict, in the face of adversity. This is because of his firsthand experience of the atrocities of war and dictatorship. In addition to losing family and friends in the war, the Taylor regime jailed and exiled Sirleaf, and tore down *The Daily Talk* shack twice.

Sirleaf claims that *The Daily Talk*'s coverage of the government's response to Ebola moved them to take more active measures, constructing emergency treatment units around the country and supporting other preventative services. 'I think the scorecard of *The Daily Talk* prompted action [on Ebola] by the government as it was seen worldwide. We exposed government weaknesses,' he explains.

Sirleaf explains that in Liberia, 'The readers [of *The Daily Talk*] wanted to know about the symptoms of Ebola. They wanted to know the mechanisms to prevent Ebola, the source of the virus, and if it was created by humans.'

Sirleaf is working to expand the scope of *The Daily Talk* billboard's content. In 2013, funded and mentored by my organization, the Accountability Lab, he began to include a section with step-by-step instructions on how to navigate government services, such as how to register a business, obtain a birth certificate, get a new passport, or submit a Freedom of Information request. This section also directly served people's needs for information about Ebola.

'We expect the change to be that citizens better understand how to engage with government constructively and better understand where processes may be going wrong,' says Lawrence Yealue, our country director in Liberia – which is why the Lab now hopes to work with *The Daily Talk* to expand even further.

During the Ebola crisis, the civic education section of *The Daily Talk* covered the location of hospitals and Ebola treatment units in Monrovia, best practices on sanitation and hygiene, and how to report suspected Ebola cases. And what is the symbol Sirleaf used for the deadly disease? How does he portray Ebola to help people make sense of it? A devil with a pitchfork.

Accountapreneurs: An entrepreneurial approach to accountability

Governments around the world have shown an impressive ability to pass transparency laws, set up anti-corruption organizations and implement public financial management reforms, while remaining deeply unaccountable to their citizens. This is where crucial leaders like Alfred Sirleaf come in.

But, perhaps counter-intuitively, international donors' financial systems and large-scale project management practices can also further enable, rather than eliminate, corruption. In many aid agencies, there are incentives for managers to spend significant amounts of resources quickly, rather than effectively. The huge amounts of money foreign governments pour into poor countries often do not ensure success nor change, and actually pervert incentives. In some cases, NGOs pop up to write proposals and sub-contract for projects, tapping into these funding flows as part of a business proposition rather than an authentic effort to generate positive social and economic change.

Progress is being made – in recent years there have been some important steps forward in terms of donor and NGO transparency, oversight mechanisms, and understandings of accountability. But despite many fantastic people working within aid agencies and civil society organizations, there is still a long way to go – incentives are not always structured in a way that encourages risk-taking or learning from failure. At best we repeat the mistakes of the past, and at worst we become an expensive part of precisely the unaccountable systems we set out to change.

Moreover, in enhancing local leadership and governance around the world, there is often an implicit assumption that making information more transparent leads to greater accountability, which is by no means the case. The information has to be useful and usable for citizens – which is the key thing that Alfred Sirleaf is doing in Liberia.

There is also confusion at times between financial accountability (corruption) and the broader notion of accountability as it relates to the relationships between power-holders, the structures of power, and citizens. If a school needs to be built or repaired in a community, for example, the problem generally is not that the money or technical skills are not available, it is that systems of accountability have not been put in place to allow citizens to decide upon or monitor the process of building that school. Corruption is a symptom of a lack of accountability, not a cause, and cannot be conceived of in isolation from the conditions that bring it about.

So what can outsiders do to help build healthier, more responsive government services in poor countries? At the heart of this is an approach that focuses on justice and fairness. 'The key,' says Thomas Tweh, a community leader in the West Point neighbourhood of Monrovia, 'is that disputes are resolved in accountable and sustainable ways' (Glencorse, 2014).

Tweh has a vision for dealing with justice issues at the local level in Liberia, where the formal legal system can often be slow, over-burdened, expensive, and corrupt. Tweh does not avoid the system, however, but collaborates with the police and commissioner's office to refer cases downwards from the courts to a community grievance-redress mechanism.

Tweh trains volunteer mediators to serve on community justice teams that resolve disputes by building trust and understanding among the parties. The entire community is made aware of this free service through the deployment of a town crier, who makes the rounds of the community every day to remind people to use the mediation service for whatever issues they face – from divorce to theft to a business deal gone sour. By handling cases locally, the community justice teams reduce the burden on the formal legal system and, even more importantly, save citizens time and money better used to earn a living.

Getting more creative with the tools deployed to build accountability means focusing on context. We started an 'accountability incubator' in Liberia to identify – through a competitive process – accountapreneurs (individuals or groups that demonstrate an entrepreneurial approach to accountability issues, and who are smart risks) like Thomas Tweh and Alfred Sirleaf. The incubator provides all the support these changemakers need to make their ideas work over time, including training, mentorship, networks, communications support and seed funding (of between $1,000–10,000).

The results for the community justice teams have been impressive. The outcome is a process that merges formal and informal tools for accountability and justice in a manner that is seen to be fair and equitable by the community, saving time, money and effort. In their first year, the community justice teams resolved almost 80 cases without any recidivism. This saved the parties involved almost 500,000 Liberian dollars ($5,000) in fees (and bribes) and approximately 350 days of time that people would have been engaged in legal proceedings. All this for an investment of just $3,000.

The small grants process itself helps citizens to think in new ways about how best to make powerholders of different types accountable. In West Point, citizens now have begun to discuss how the community mediation process could be integrated with other branches of government. New volunteers are being brought on board to help facilitate the process. In other communities, similar community justice teams have now emerged to mediate local conflicts in similar ways. This is extremely small scale, of course, but it is the basis for real trust-building and social cohesion. It is the platform from which accountability can grow.

Box 14.1 Briefcase NGOs: how widespread are they, really?

By Jennifer Lentfer

> *Definition of a briefcase (or suitcase) NGO: A fraudulent non-profit organization, set up by only one or two persons, only to obtain money from donors but having no programmes on the ground.*

I have long suspected that the phenomena of briefcase NGOs is not as widespread as purported. Anecdotal evidence, e.g. 'I knew this guy,' is told and re-told in the international-aid sector, and in the process becomes elevated to be considered 'typical', creating an image problem for all non-profits in poor countries, even when we know that the number and diversity of civil-society organizations in any one country is great.

I also suspect some funders have deeper issues with briefcase NGOs than others due to their 'partnership' approach. Researcher Eugenia Lee (2013, 2014) has been thoughtfully writing about this phenomenon recently, raising the question as to whether foreign aid itself has driven the rise of briefcase NGOs and perverted the non-profit incentive structure in countries receiving international assistance.

Indigenous grassroots groups embedded at the community level may lack the required accountability mechanisms and sophisticated processes that would make them more recog-nizable or esteemed in the development sector, but they have a range of capacities and competencies that also distinguish them from other civil-society actors – resourcefulness, deep contextual knowledge, community embeddedness, language and cultural capacities, and the ability to operate in a responsive manner to local needs – and which are those that international NGOs and donors lack. In the meantime, most 'old-school' project-based funding mechanisms and proposal/reporting procedures continue to be so risk-averse that they can easily be exploited by nefarious characters.

Unfortunately I continue to hear briefcase NGOs used as an excuse for larger agencies not to alter or expand their proposal/reporting procedures so that more local organiza-tions can take part. True accountability is rarely found on paper and the most effective grassroots organizations and movements I know ensure that the communities they serve are ultimately the judge of their success. Funders need to develop funding mechanisms that will increase NGOs' responsiveness and resourcefulness, rather than distract them from their constituencies. It is indeed possible for diligent and thoughtful people to separate the wheat from the chaff.

Regardless of how widespread the phenomena of briefcase NGOs may be (or not be), aid and philanthropic wealth can be better distributed to reach everyday people. We need a larger and more diverse section of people working on behalf of the common good.

As accountapreneurs like Thomas Tweh and Alfred Sirleaf demonstrate, building accountability is a process that can grow from citizens themselves, if provided with the right kinds of support over time. And in our incubator, if a seemingly good idea does not prove to be quite as successful as hoped, the process of thinking about alternative solutions may in turn lead to important lessons learned and new ideas. The financial input of small grants is minimal, making the risks even smarter.

Summary points

- Accountability is dependent on building trust, which can only be done locally, over time.

- There is also confusion at times between financial accountability (corruption) and the broader notion of accountability as it relates to the relationships between powerholders, the structures of power, and citizens.
- Information, made available in ways that enable local people to access and understand it, can help people hold their government accountable.
- Getting more creative with the tools deployed to build accountability means focusing on context. By supporting local leaders, outsiders can more directly address issues of inclusion and fairness.

About the author

Blair Glencorse is founder and executive director of Accountability Lab <http://www.accountabilitylab.org> in Washington DC, USA.

CHAPTER 15

Out of the comfort zone: Addressing the needs of women's rights defenders

Keely Tongate

Transgressing social norms that deny women's rights is not for the weak of heart.

Luiza,[2] an activist I have known since 2007, has seen many attempts at silencing her voice in her home of Chechnya. As part of her work helping women survivors of state-sponsored violence, Luiza herself encounters regular violence and intimidation. There was the car with tell-tale tinted windows and no number plates that tried to run over her sister after she gave a speech attacking Chechnya's poor human-rights record. The constant emergency trips to neighbouring republics with her children after facing threats from gangs on the government payroll, those trying to keep activists in check by scaring them into submission. For Luiza, and too many women defenders, the targeting of children is a well-practiced tactic.

For most, activism is a lifelong journey, much of which goes unrecognized by larger society. Yet, along the way, there are flashes in the pan, certain tactics or campaigns that provoke the ire of those in power. In these situations, the risks are real and, too often, life-threatening. Nimble and responsive grants help ensure activists on the front lines stay safe.

For Luiza, less than $5,000 from the Urgent Action Fund for Women's Human Rights (UAF) allowed her to relocate to a safer city with her family so she could continue her women's rights work in the long term. A non-responsive grant funding Luiza's advocacy activities would have left Luiza to face her fate without the safety net that responsive grants provide. A grant lacking a gendered approach, which only allowed for Luiza's relocation but not her family's, would have denied her family responsibility and forced her to find the additional funds to bring them with her.

When a crisis or new opportunity arises, women and trans*[3] activists need effective, quick, and innovative ways to respond. Often, they are unable to implement these strategic interventions due to a lack of flexible funds, or due to the lengthy approval processes of many donors. In these cases, small, timely grants, with few bureaucratic strings attached, can have great impact.

http://dx.doi.org/10.3362/9781780449302.015

How can responsive grantmaking address gender inequality?

Traditional funding for gender projects often targets the symptoms of gender inequality, as the cause of the disease is much harder to pinpoint. Instead of challenging oppressive structures, including family, that stifle women's ability to be full participants in both public and private spheres, funders choose safe and palatable projects that don't stray too far from societal conceptions of women and the requisite intersection with motherhood. Examples include countless programmes that 'empower' women to become financial actors without dissecting the power inequities bound up in traditional roles and decision-making around financial resources at the household or societal level.

Funding for clinics to prevent infant and mother mortality are necessary and *do* save lives. But what about projects that target the phenomenon of sex-selective infanticide? India's 2011 census is clear: for children 0–6 years, the gender ratio is 914 girls to 1,000 boys. This means that for every 1,000 boys, at least 60–70 girls are killed, the most imbalanced gender ratio since India's independence in 1947. (The 50 Million Missing Campaign, 2011) There is no quick fix to combatting sexual and gender-based violence; insidious cultural norms seeped in history and intersecting with other forms of oppression (class, caste, sexuality, disability, etc.) infect our planet.

While I understand the clarity and comfort that funding impact and tracking lives saved offers, it's not enough. There are vibrant organizations and movements that are tackling the disease of gender inequality, community by community. For example, whether it's creating a bullying-free space for gender non-conforming children in the US, or drafting legislation that recognizes trans* people's right to legally identify their gender as different to that assigned at birth, trans* activism is severely underfunded. According to a recent international survey, out of 340 trans* or intersex organizations, half have a budget of less than $10,000. (Eisfeld et al., 2013)

UAF was founded to meet this need for flexible, responsive grants. UAF's activist-led philosophy is inherently flexible and responsive to changing circumstances. We believe that there is not a one-size-fits-all approach to social change, and that impacted communities are the best judges of strategy. A flexible and responsive approach also recognizes that challenging oppressive systems often results in violent backlash. With this grounding, we trust that activists have the strategy and merely lack the flexible funds to take advantage of critical windows of opportunity for their advocacy or to stay safe when facing backlash.

UAF's maximum grant is only $5,000, yet activists have leveraged these resources for great impact. In the Kurdish region of Turkey, a vocal women's rights organization, critical of government policies towards the Kurdish population, was targeted using anti-terrorism legislation. With the quick mobilization of funds to bring women from across Turkey to stand witness and show solidarity during the trial, the case was dropped. From Egypt to Ukraine and Afghanistan, revolutions and rapidly changing political contexts require a flexible and responsive approach for activists poised to make or protect hard-won gains, while countering backlash.

A common assumption about international philanthropy is that responsive strategies belong only to chaotic, emergency-response situations, while proactive strategies belong in more stable contexts, where long-term funding is available. I have learned that neither of these assumptions is entirely true. In fact, funders must be prepared to implement both proactive and responsive strategies, especially in difficult and rapidly-changing contexts.

Being proactive in rapidly changing contexts

Responsive grantmaking means moving out of our comfort zone as funders, listening to advisors who are addressing the root of problems in their localities. We understand strategies are contextual; we are there to listen, learn and take the lessons back into our own communities to advance the human rights of all people, regardless of gender identity. Sixteen years of experience demonstrates that small, responsive grants are a critical component of supporting women's and trans* human rights defenders and movements.

However, it is not enough. The deteriorating security situation that impedes activists' ability to advance a human-rights agenda requires attention from funders. UAF has developed a rich store of institutional knowledge on the strategies and needs of women's and trans* human rights activists, and the contexts in which they work. And because we provide rapid grants with quick turnaround we can integrate new knowledge of emerging trends impacting activists in real time.

Women activists face gendered threats that often blur the line between personal and public spaces. To address this, in collaboration with activists and colleague organizations, UAF developed 'integrated security' training that accounts for the gendered nature of threats.

For example, the Kremlin-appointed president of Chechnya, Ramzan Kadirov, introduced a plan for 'moral education' in 2008, which included a decree requiring that all women employed in the state sector, and all female school and university students, must wear headscarves. Kadirov's men enforced this decree by shooting girls that had their heads uncovered with paintball guns, physically marking them out for surveillance and public scrutiny. A woman's choice to cover (or not) her head and the backlash this causes has a particular gendered component.

UAF's integrated security training melds practical security prevention, creating security plans, and digital security, with space for activists like Luiza to reflect and enhance their toolkit of methods to increase their overall safety and well-being. Integrated security training is a response to a gap in support for women's rights activists to effectively manage and plan for future insecurity. UAF also provided proactive funding to allow Luiza and colleagues to attend just such a workshop after providing her and other activists in Chechnya with responsive security grants. In this way, funding integrated security is both proactive and responsive to the needs of Chechen women activists.

The training is context specific. For activists in Chechnya, creating individual and organizational security plans, for example, ensures that if one woman is threatened, there are others standing by to help to keep her safe. A security plan provides more options when things get especially dangerous, such as when the car with tinted windows is heading in your direction. Sending regular texts when traveling to remote villages ensures that someone knows where Chechen activists are at all times, in case of (un)expected trouble. In this system, when one person struggles, others are mobilized to support them.

Supporting the collective also diffuses risks to leaders by shoring up the capacity of other members of the community, thereby strengthening groups of individuals as a movement. Activists are more resilient when they do not stand alone. As Luiza told me: 'Before I never even thought about self-care, but since I started to participate at the trainings on security, I've understood its importance. If you go without rest, one day you will not be able to continue what you do.'

Can we be both proactive and responsive funders?

Nimble and timely funding that is inherently flexible supports movements to adapt as necessary to changing circumstances and contexts. Small responsive grants are the core of what UAF does. Yet, given the reality and precariousness of the risks women's human-rights defenders face, we are forced to move beyond a responsive approach. UAF has developed proactive funding mechanisms via strategies like integrated security workshops that give activists the tools they need to stay safe so they can continue their work advancing women's and trans* human rights for the long term. This is a means of scaling up UAF's support beyond a focus on threatened individuals. A localized approach, supporting mutually reinforcing networks of activists, strengthens movements. This strategy provides activists with the confidence necessary to tackle deeply-rooted gender inequality, knowing that backlash will not be absorbed individually, but as a collective.

Advisors and grantees are critical partners in shaping our programmatic priorities and process. We are committed to maintaining accountability to the women's and trans* movements we support. From evaluating all grant proposals, to informing programmatic priorities, regional advisors are the backbone and heart of our work. This model allows impacted communities to evaluate the significance of small grants in real time. This activist-led approach also highlights gaps in UAF's responsive funding model, allowing us to make space for proactive funding to support safer women's and trans* movements.

We believe that the best way to support activists seeking to affect systemic change is to adopt a flexible, adaptive grantmaking approach that supports the creativity and vision of women's and trans* movements. This is because activists are constantly devising new methods for creating change. Flexible grantmaking, informed by local activists, whether proactive or responsive, allows activists to innovate and respond to unanticipated situations as they arise.

Box 15.1 A new kind of funder: Four things they do differently

By Jennifer Lentfer

Lengthy proposals, onerous reporting, and heavy-handed financial mechanisms frankly cannot offer useful capital to organizations that don't fit the 'high-capacity' mould of international aid and philanthropy, let alone emerging social movements. To change this, this new kind of funder will do four things better than traditional donors still stuck in the old ways of moving money around:

1. They are patient.

They invest not just today's services or activities, but allow for uncertainty and potentially fewer short-term results in favour of long-term outcomes.

2. Their money follows ideas and people, rather than activities.

Projects may be the modus operandi, but funders do not allow them define or confine relationships.

3. They demonstrate a tolerance for risk, rather than failure.

They help keep a focus on results, yet offer flexibility and responsiveness to changing conditions.

4. They are able and willing to look within.

They examine how their own policies and practices exclude and/or inhibit some of the most innovative and effective organizations.

Financing for social change can no longer be disconnected from people and place, or flow into a community based on a funder's imperatives. A new kind of funder is courageous enough to put their partners' needs first – so that both can adapt to arising needs, inherent complexities, and local realities. A new kind of funder knows that serving their partners' interests first is what will ultimately fulfil their own.

Summary points

- Responsive grantmaking for activists saves lives. In times of crisis or when a new opportunity arises, small, timely grants, with few bureaucratic strings attached, can have great impact.
- Gendered threats to activists require special attention. For example, support to women or trans* activists can be bound up in traditional roles that may be unknown to outsiders.
- Proactive grants can build support networks for activists so they are prepared, flexible, and empowered to address emergency situations when they arise.

About the author

Keely Tongate is coordinator of Philanthropy Advancing Women's Human Rights (PAWHR). She worked at Urgent Action Fund from 2006–2014, as programme officer and then director of programmes.

CHAPTER 16
Fruitful failures and the pull of curiosity

Marc Maxmeister

Here was my dilemma. The typical organization using GlobalGiving's online giving website gets less than US$5,000 a year through our website. In its 16-year existence, GlobalGiving has supported over 15,000 projects by enabling individual givers, primarily in the US and the UK, to find and support vetted local organizations in 165 countries around the world.

How in the heck were we supposed to evaluate the multitude of organizations we support? They work everywhere. They do everything.

You see, GlobalGiving *guarantees* every donation; if a person gives to an organization and months or years later is unhappy with the organization, GlobalGiving gives them the money back to reallocate to another organization of their choice. This commitment keeps us honest as 'microgrant-makers' who must select organizations that honour their promises to funders. Such guarantees earn trust.

We knew that 'doing evaluations' for 32,000+ organizations would need to be different than the approaches that big aid funders use. Typically, if a foundation gives grants in $100,000 or $500,000 chunks, they'll audit the recipient. They'll send out professional observers to confirm that things in a village match what the recipient promised. And this third party ultimately decides whether the project 'worked'. We needed a more low-cost approach, and a more honest one. The real hidden cost of evaluations in the aid world isn't the price tag for site visits – it is that so few evaluations reveal the underlying problems, most importantly, the dissatisfaction of the people the project or organization was intending to help. People are the experts on whether they are being well-served, and delivering better results in the future will require every organization to think about how it learns and how it drives down the cost of its own learning.

After an experience with a GlobalGiving partner's negative feedback loop leading to the Kenyan youth soccer organization's dismantling and demise (see my essay, 'What "real-time" community feedback can tell you that evaluations can't', page 122 for the full story), we knew that if we could gather honest feedback, it would be invaluable. We wrote up this experience as a case study and the Rockefeller Foundation supported a larger experiment on how we could give more people this kind of voice on a regional level.

This was the beginning of our GlobalGiving Storytelling Project. At the time, we had no standard evaluation process because none of the off-the-shelf

http://dx.doi.org/10.3362/9781780449302.016

options would ever have worked for our situation. Rockefeller gave us an opportunity to try something new, not because we had a solution in hand, but because we were listening and flexible.

And so the GlobalGiving Storytelling Project was born. The project asked people in communities all across East Africa to tell a story about a time when a person or organization tried to help someone or change something in their community. From 2010 to 2013, over 60,000 stories were collected in Kenya and Uganda by scribes who interview people they know and write the stories down on paper and then transcribe. The approach generates a massive, continuous story collection through thousands of people, and smart visual tools that help people see patterns and discuss their various interpretations about whether changes are occurring. Then non-profits can use this information to see if they are making the difference they suppose – from the crowd-sourced perspective of the general public.

As the leader of the Storytelling Project, my definition of the project's success is seeing organizations making decisions that are in part informed by community knowledge. When an organization can describe some action they took that they would have not otherwise taken without feedback in the form of community stories, this is a significant way for GlobalGiving to know we have been successful as a funder.

But that's *not* the perspective with which we started out. Unfortunately nobody wants to read about all the failures, so I share a tidier story.

Understanding the problem you are trying to solve

The first step when we started was to turn to the organizations themselves. We asked a group of our partners in East Africa to each round up a dozen young people that we would meet and train as scribes. These scribes went out with two-page paper surveys, interviewed community members, and collected stories about a person or organization trying to do something to help the community. This prototype idea went through *many* iterations in the first four months.

We collected 2,500 stories in that pilot year, through a labour-intensive process. Everything was written first then retyped into web forms later, but it worked. By contrast, every subsequent paperless-technology version of this experiment failed. We tried smart phones, SMS messaging, voice recorders, and computer labs. We were promised smart pens and survey software on tablets but they never arrived in time. Rather than stick to the original design, we changed things to fit what seemed to be working.

That year we did every part of the storytelling process in discrete steps. We announced the idea to partners, trained people, collected stories, transcribed thousands of handwritten pages, plugged these narratives and their associated survey questions into proprietary software, generated conclusions, and then met to discuss the findings with local NGOs.

But when the pilot ended, the process had to be redesigned to scale. That's why 'pilot' and 'scaling up' are such contentious buzzwords. Funders want to fund pilots that have scalability; communities want successful pilots to continue permanently.

Pilots rarely scale up without many cost-cutting design changes because the experiments to find out what works will always be more expensive to run than the streamlined, scalable final design. I call these the 'scientific phase' and the 'engineering phase'. Funders have started to fund these separately, with separate teams reviewing applications for each phase, but designing both a highly effective solution and a cost-effective scalable one takes many iterations, and the funding should be structured to support both science and engineering phases.

Accomplishing more with less

In our second year (the engineering phase), we ran the same experiment again but on a continuous basis, with every step happening concurrently. So instead of five organizations and five locations, we were managing 40 organizations – recruiting, training, collecting, transcribing, and analyzing at all times. We were still running a prototype-sized budget: only three times more money to manage ten times more work.

This is typical design engineering for scaling up – the kind where we learn how to accomplish more with less (needless to say, much like visionary leaders working in resource-poor environments). Many projects break when they try to scale up because efficiency does not come from size; it comes from improving each step in a process.

In my case, it made the most sense for me to learn to be a programmer, because that allowed us run more experiments and refine each step in the process. Looking back, I realize I was filling up my skills toolbox so fast that by the time I'd finished managing the project, the budget wouldn't have been big enough to afford someone who started with all my skills! What I embraced as professional development packed the bigger skill set into a lean budget.

Driving the cost of learning down

Many new process problems emerged when we started running the programme continuously. All stories needed to be geocoded, so we built an automatic system for that.

Then, because our solicitation of community stories is so truly open-ended, hundreds of unknown organizations were named every month. These organization names needed to be cleaned up and linked to the people at those institutions that could respond to the feedback. We employed a mix of software and humans to keep the task manageable.

Geocoding stories and organizational name clean-up are examples of systems that accelerated the 'datafication' of a real world problem. Datafication is a process of turning human readable notes, documents, recordings, and papers into machine readable data, with a consistent structure and metadata – added context data – alongside the 'raw' data. Datafication is what makes innovation affordable, because modern algorithms can thoroughly exploit the full depth of information for understanding a problem for a fraction of what professional statisticians and evaluators cost. Neither solution is perfect (we correctly geocoded about 90 per cent of stories and resolved organization names for 66 per cent of stories), but they required an hour a month of staff time to manage, instead of the 30-plus hours we spent doing this in the pilot. Datafication is what makes innovation affordable, and yet few organizational leaders recognize this.

Testing, testing, testing ... and more testing

I believe the power of storytelling and community feedback comes through the insights that local organizations glean from them. In other words, stories have no value if nobody is listening. But after a year in the engineering phase, scribes had collected over 30,000 stories from about 50 locations in Kenya and Uganda, but hardly any of our GlobalGiving's partner organizations were using them in their project design and evaluations.

So our focus shifted in year three from getting tens of thousands of community stories to getting organizations and communities to listen. We tried to build functional citizen-organization feedback loops out of our story data, but failed in many ways. We tried a series of face-to-face community meetings where we delivered personalized digests of local stories to each organization. These were well attended but nobody took any demonstrable action as a result. We tried the positive deviance model, whereby we would recognize the behaviour of local organizations that were listening and acting, aligned with local needs. We tried a Clinton Global Initiative model, where organizations would select follow-up tasks and return to report on their progress (and rise in prestige among their peer organizations at meetings).

Even though organizations rated the importance of community voice in their decision-making as a nine on a scale of one to ten in surveys, none of these approaches worked. Actions always speak louder than words, and our feedback system was not prompting action.

After five months of testing failed face-to-face strategies, we decided to pivot our approach. I tried using SMS (text messaging) to engage citizens and actors directly. Perhaps individuals would drive the feedback loop where institutions would not?

I tested a half dozen commercial text-messaging systems before deciding to build my own with the features I really needed. I ran several experiments with it to see if community scribes, organizations, or storytellers would be interested in receiving messages and responding about topics that interested them.

I built an SMS-based evaluation tool for an organization member to use, but none of these worked. The response rate to some of these offerings was as low as 2 per cent, but it was 66 per cent for our scribes – an important discovery for later.

Despite the need to pivot twice in eight months, we were actually getting more efficient. Testing two complete paradigms for how feedback loops ought to work was fruitful. We'd carried an idea through a structured process and engaged all the right people in a collaborative experiment. We had spent most of our time testing theories of change where less innovative organizations would merely deliberate over the wording of their precious 'theory of change' documents.

Unceasing evolution

So what should we try next? I revisited the few organizations that did find our storytelling useful. Each of them was rooted in a community and had already shown evidence of responding to community needs before they joined GlobalGiving. All we were doing was making that innate focus easier to manage. Each had a core programme that it managed well and one or more smaller programmes that had evolved to meet a community need. The Trans-Nzoia Youth Sports Association in Kitale, Kenya, for example, had involved the elders in counselling at-risk youth, and had worked to lower teen school-dropout rates, which was beyond its original mission. Vijana Amani Pamoja (Peace-Youth-Together) in Nairobi had added an after-school programme for adolescent girls that had nothing to do with sports or HIV, its core mission.

I spent more time understanding how these organizations worked in order to build simpler and more focused visualizations of the stories that served their needs. I pivoted towards user-centred design. What I found was that, even though GlobalGiving needed a storytelling method that would map to any kind of community effort worldwide, each organization needed it to answer more specific questions about the communities they served. Here are a few:

- Why are adolescents running away from home and ending up in the nearest city?
- What social factors appear in these stories?
- What issues do 8 to 14 year old girls face each day in Kamukunji, a Nairobi slum?
- How do men and women describe food security around Lake Victoria?
- What social issues prevent girls in Kisii from attending a school that specifically prevents them from undergoing female genital mutilation?
- How does organization X's rape prevention programme compare with a better funded one by USAID?
- Are there any clever solutions to the pervasive problem of lack of funds for school fees?
- What kinds of people discriminate against people living with HIV?

The engaged organizations wanted tools to answer these questions, so we focused on how best to analyse the stories for them. We still didn't know how we could turn a lot of data into meaningful conclusions for hundreds of organizations. We had begun by licensing software for this task, but by our third year we knew that it wasn't suited to our purpose. It would never answer the kinds of questions organizations were asking.

The purpose is project was evolving far away from our original idea of a tool to measure impact. Instead of finding the organizations that didn't listen to their community (and therefore might cost us money as we honour our 100 per cent donor-satisfaction guarantee), we were amplifying finding the ones that *did* listen well and were curious about the root causes of complex social problems.

Story-centred learning

Our story collection method has become more flexible so that the data can satisfy the curiosity of any organization on any topic, but with enough structure to generate benchmarking and quantitative trending at 10 per cent of the cost of a traditional evaluation. Our best organizations seemed open to learning from stories with our help. As a result, we developed tools for them. Curiosity, it turns out, is one of the three hallmark characteristics of successful social-change organizations and movements, as I outline in my book, *Storytelling for Change* (Maxmeister, 2017).

These tools haven't caught on like wildfire, but because they are online, we can track who uses them, and how often, and follow up. Herein lies the change accelerator in this whole process: because we can finally track the way people interact with our feedback tools, we can start to understand the thinking within organizations. This behaviour is a better reflection of an organization's worldview than any mission statement. We now mitigate our risk as a funder by reverse engineering what motivates people to do the work they do in and for a community.

This is what datafication is all about – practically free ongoing experiments that constantly update our understanding as we iterate. Every day the system would email me a report of who used what tool to ask what question and when, from anywhere in the world. And by year six, we were getting deep insights into the types of work that truly matters most to the people affected by poverty in East Africa.

Tracking the *reaction* that organizations have to this information about themselves and the communities where they work (or about some complex social problem to address) tells us much more about each organization than the stories themselves. It's a way of quantifying organizational curiosity, and curious organizations are more likely to be innovators, community-focused, and quick learners.

In many ways we're back to square one of the piloting phase, because we've changed the question. We began by asking how we gather a ton of community feedback to determine an organization's impact. But the question became, 'how do we deliver knowledge back to those who can use it to make their world better?'

Turns out, there are rules to making your experiment consistently yield valuable lessons. And they show us that learning the most from experiments is actually more of a cycle:

1. Understand the problem.
2. Plan to iterate your design.
3. Optimize to drive down the cost of learning.
4. Focus on cheaper datafication.
5. Never stop testing your assumptions.

GO BACK TO 1.

Conclusion

If my story has a moral it is this: The only place you'll find innovative solutions is after a long line of failures. Anyone who claims otherwise is lying, or even worse, a thief who stole the brilliant solution from some uncredited worker struggling in the tar pits of problem solving.

So after six years and 60,000 stories, are we any closer to an answer? Can we inform communities and decision makers in a meaningful way? Can citizens eventually manage small-scale projects themselves with our feedback?

At first glance, the answer would seem to be no. Six years out, few organizations use the community feedback tools we offer them. With these behaviours so rarely rewarded in traditional aid and philanthropy, why would we expect to find curious, innovative, grassroots-led organizations?

But there are a few curious organizations out there getting value out of it – taking risks, challenging their own assumptions, and talking openly about all their failures. Each year that the GlobalGiving Storytelling Project employed this fruitful failures mindset, we were able to test more and learn more rapidly than the previous one. Because this learning focus has worked for us, I believe it will work for other curiosity-driven organizations. In years four and five, we pivoted to testing ways to reward organizational curiosity. Those that achieved the best results on the ground were the curious ones who listened intently and transformed their understanding of their purpose along the way. So perhaps the barrier to listening isn't new mechanisms for feedback, but our own resistance to growth? We believe so.

The short version of our big theory is: *Listen. Act. Learn. Repeat.* It is painted on the wall at GlobalGiving and I believe this belongs on the wall of every organization that wants to solve complex social problems. Philanthropy doesn't suffer from a lack of money; it starves from a lack of transformative listening and iterative learning.

Summary points

- Local people are the experts on whether they are being well-served.
- Storytelling can inform learning and iteration of strategy rather than purely measurement impact.
- Evaluation systems can be created to collect information from the people being served and to assist the grassroots organization to improve their programmes and systems.
- The only place you'll find innovative solutions is after a long line of failures. It is necessary for organizational development and evolution.

About the author

Marc Maxmeister is chief innovation officer at Keystone Accountability <http://keystoneaccountability.org> in Washington, DC. He created and managed GlobalGiving's <https://www.globalgiving.org> Storytelling Project from 2009 to 2015 and from it built the data analysis tools at storylearning. org <http://storylearning.org/>.

CHAPTER 17

What if we saw 'mistakes' as fuel for innovation?[4]

Rajasvini Bhansali

A few years ago, a Guatemalan organization called the Women's Association for the Development of Sacatepéquez (AFEDES), discovered something troubling: its programmes were not making much of an impact. AFEDES was founded in 1998 by a group of Maya Kak'chiquel women to address the problem of chronic malnutrition and lack of educational opportunities among children and women of the department[5] of Sacatepequez following the Guatemalan civil war. To promote economic opportunity, AFEDES also developed a robust microcredit, savings and loans, financial management, and income-generating skills-building programme.

However, they began to see that some women were deeper in debt at the end of the programme than at the start. Women were not participating as actively outside their homes as AFEDES had hoped. Inside their homes, nutrition levels were not improving. In fact, more women were approaching AFEDES to ask for support around domestic violence than for economic concerns. Milvian Aspuac, interim director of AFEDES (quoted in italics below and throughout), explains:

> *We realized the importance of promoting the rights of women as they were continually violated at every level. It was necessary for [us as] women to regain our self-esteem, know our rights, stop violence against us. We realized that, as women, we did not feed ourselves well. We produced just to sell, not thinking about the family consumption. We were sick. Conventional agricultural practices are polluting the environment. We live in a world where money is the main thing. Women's caring work is not valued. So we began to work for our freedom and autonomy.*

Revealing no single solution

AFEDES had been a Thousand Currents (formerly IDEX) grant partner since 2005. At the time we started our partnership, microcredit was seen by many in the international aid and philanthropic community as a magic bullet to eradicate poverty. But in 2006 and 2007, the women of AFEDES had looked deeper and come to an important conclusion: women's oppression could not

http://dx.doi.org/10.3362/9781780449302.017

be solved by credit alone. In fact, all human development indicators in the community pointed to increasing women's disempowerment.

> *We realized that the problems we face are structural, and that they deal with patriarchy, capitalism and colonialism; our actions ... had contradictions and inconsistencies in relation to the economic enterprises. We believed that they somehow responded to the principles of capitalism, and actually did not contribute much to women's [well-being].*

In a bold and deliberate move, AFEDES set out to examine the root causes of these troubling results. Through this inquiry, AFEDES was willing to be wrong, to learn from mistakes, and to realign programmes with community needs. AFEDES, as a community-led organization, changed its entire programmatic focus based on what it learned from this process of reflection.

> *We decided to operate in line with our new thinking and political commitment, to move toward a new economy (or rather return to or recall the principles and ancestral practices of our grandparents, what we now call food sovereignty). In the short term, we decided to walk together towards an organic farming training process, and later solidarity with feminist economics that question the sexual division of a labour economy. Later we started talking about economic alternatives and income-generating initiatives as resistance.*

This process of self-reflection was not easy. It was easy to show donors superficial success from AFEDES' microcredit programme. What they now were embarking upon was a non-linear process of social transformation that would require, first and foremost, meaningful community accountability.

Risking innovation from within

So AFEDES started a new, 18-week programme to empower indigenous women by educating and informing them about the legal and social mechanisms that exist to protect them from injustice. Other funders turned away from AFEDES for this risky new venture.

> *We talked about the importance of redirecting the microcredit portfolio to projects that help women to pursue their economic autonomy, being careful not to follow the logic of capitalism. We also decided to strengthen the ethnic identity of AFEDES as a Kaqchikeles women's organization. This change led to the departure of many [funding] partners who only wanted to continue to offer banking services, which had a very high cost to AFEDES, both organizationally and financially.*

We at Thousand Currents stayed the course during this time for AFEDES, because that is what partnership means to us. Like AFEDES, we were willing to learn what wasn't obvious. The mutuality of our relationship dictated that we trust the analysis and strategy of our grassroots partner rather than impose our own agenda on them.

Today, AFEDES is successfully training women to become community organizers and has won major policy victories in advocating for a rural women's shelter specifically for indigenous women in the region and protection of intellectual property for their Mayan-weaving textiles designs from foreign fashion companies.

> *Our aspiration is the Utz K'aslemal, or 'Buen Vivir', which means a full life, of happiness. More than 500 years ago, it was broken by the imposition of a Western culture, come to blot out all our knowledge, history, and science, thus causing a great imbalance in the web of life. From the Mayan worldview, women have a special importance in restoring that balance, because we are intimately related to life, nature, and the cosmos, which is a different way of seeing the world.*

Box 17.1 Four things to offer other than solutions

By Jennifer Lentfer

Yes, you could provide 'solutions' to this or that problem in the global South. But should that be your role? When building relationships and trust, what if instead you offered something else – your full presence, your patience, and willingness to listen? This creates the space for four things to occur:

1. You create the space for safety and acceptance.

Whatever is going on in someone's mind, whatever the circumstances, wherever they are at – good or bad – it's okay. People can bring their whole self to the space between you, where nothing is at risk of rejection. They can reveal where they feel stuck. It's important, because without this, change isn't possible.

2. You create the space for story.

We are always forming narratives, but it is only in sharing them that they gain and lose their power over us. I was honoured to interview Nobel Prize Winner Leymah Gbowee for International Women's Day in 2014. She shared with me that the first time she told the story of what happened to her and her family during the Liberian civil war, it took three hours. Only after this story was shared, she said, could she ask, 'What next?'

3. You create the space for possibility and expansion.

Sometimes, especially when I'm struggling, I have a hard time seeing the options in front of me. Then someone asks me a question, a really good question. A path that seemingly wasn't there before suddenly opens up. We are invited to grapple, navigate, wrestle deeply. People become unstuck. Doubt fades.

4. You create the space for collaboration.

Putting our skills and passions together and having fun, sounds pretty great. It is. Our shared work is pretty much the same. It's about planning, organizing, strategizing, responding – together.

Why do grassroots grantmakers tend to these spaces? Because we know struggle. Because we take inspiration from our own circumstances. Because we know intimately the timelessness and the universality of holding space for our truths to appear. Perhaps we know the courage that comes from turning towards one another and the isolation that comes from hanging desperately to our assumptions. Perhaps we've seen many, many times what happens that when a person starts to know the struggle is not just their own. The horizon reappears.

Who leads innovation and lasting change

The story of AFEDES is not just the story of what can happen when we invest in women. It is also about what can happen when we invest in and listen to the grassroots leaders and community-led organizations in our world's most marginalized communities. These people have the best understanding of the culture, history, and conditions of their own communities, and are in the best positions to address the root causes of poverty, injustice, and inequality.

As outsiders, we have to be willing to suspend judgment and our impulse toward cultural imperialism. We must resist the urge to determine what's right for others. Producing experts and expertise is not the exclusive domain of the global North. That makes it our job to learn from the groups that are social innovators in their own context. Taking their lead in imagining new and better ways will solve entrenched problems.

Most of all, the story of AFEDES was a lesson in staying the course when other funders leave. AFEDES not only changed their strategic direction, they became more grounded and committed to women's empowerment. In practice, this meant deep dedication to individual self-determination, collective resilience, and grassroots solidarity.

The problem is that staying the course with partners is not the way most international assistance is currently practiced. Instead, our own philanthropic silos and large-scale, externally-led efforts can undermine collaboration and movement-building. The results are often limited and short-lived, and groups on the frontlines, like AFEDES, don't get access to the funding they so desperately need to take risks, make mistakes, innovate, and grow.

A few years ago, Thousand Currents commissioned an external evaluation report because we wanted to hear directly from our partners about the effectiveness of our model. According to the findings, nearly 90 per cent stated they have been able to develop community-based solutions. Thousand Currents' partners are able to articulate the progress they are making locally and they are utilizing our solidarity and resources to build stronger alliances and linkages to other social-change organizations and movements in their local areas, regions and internationally.

Delighted as we are with these results – a strong endorsement for our partnership model – we also know there is much more room for growth in our journey as a learning, adaptive, flexible, and impactful grantmaker. Our work with groups like AFEDES in Guatemala reminds us of the courage and rigour of our grassroots community leaders in their quest for justice despite tremendous obstacles.

As AFEDES and our other partners around the world transform their failures into innovation, so must we.

Summary points

- Self-determination within local organizations is key to addressing root causes of injustice. Supporting organizations in their own processes of reflection leads to important changes in strategy.

- Smart risks mean acknowledging when something isn't working, and going through a process of self-reflection and realignment with local priorities will get to real impact. For example, women's oppression cannot be solved by credit alone. Issues of patriarchy, capitalism, and colonialism must also be acknowledged and addressed.
- Philanthropic silos and large-scale, externally-led efforts can undermine collaboration and movement-building. When donors can stay the course, lasting sea changes are possible.

About the author

Rajasvini Bhansali is executive director of Thousand Currents <https://www.idex.org> (formerly called IDEX - International Development Exchange) in Berkeley, California, USA.

Notes

1. Portions of this essay were originally published as 'When reliable information is gold: Demanding the truth during the Ebola epidemic' on the Oxfam Blog <https://www.oxfamamerica.org/explore/stories/when-reliable-information-is-gold-demanding-the-truth-during-the-ebola-epidemic> (posted 23 March 2015). It is used here with permission from the author.
2. Some details have been altered to preserve the anonymity of groups and individuals.
3. The Global Action for Trans* Equality (GATE) uses the term trans* to describe those people who transgress (binary) (western) gender norms, many of whom face human rights issues as a result. Trans* people include those who have a gender identity which is different to the gender assigned at birth and/or those people who feel they have to, prefer to, or choose to – whether by clothing, accessories, cosmetics or body modification – present themselves differently to the expectations of the gender role assigned to them at birth. This includes, among many others, transsexual and transgender people, transvestites, travesti, cross dressers, no gender and genderqueer people. The term trans* should be seen as a placeholder for many identities, most of which are specific to local cultures and times in history, describing people who broaden and expand a binary understanding of gender.
4. Portions of this essay were originally published as 'Restoring the balance: Radical changes in an indigenous women's group in Guatemala' by Milvian Aspuac on the IDEX Blog <https://www.idex.org/blog/2015/08/restoring-balance-radical-changes-indigenous-womens-group-guatemala> (posted 10 August 2015). It is used here with permission from the author.
5. Departments (*departamentos*) are similar to states or provinces.

References

Cotton, A. (2011) 'Paying it forward in Africa' in *The Huffington Post* [blog] <http://www.huffingtonpost.com/ann-cotton/africa-philanthropy_b_817545.html> (posted 4 February 2011; updated 25 May 2011) [accessed 26 September 2016].

Eisfeld, J., Gunther, S. and Shlasko, D. (2013) *The State of Trans* and Intersex Organizing: A case for increased support for growing but under-funded movements for human right,* Global Action for Trans* Equality (GATE) and American Jewish World Service (AJWS), Available from: <https://globaltransaction.files.wordpress.com/2014/01/trans-intersex-funding-report.pdf> [accessed 27 September 2016].

Glencorse, B. (2014) 'Putting local justice in Liberia' in *Insight on Conflict* [blog] <https://www.insightonconflict.org/blog/2014/01/liberia-local-justice> (posted 3 January 2014) [accessed on 26 September 2016].

Lee, E. (2013) 'Donor funding and briefcase NGOs' in *Local First Blog* [blog] <https://www.insightonconflict.org/blog/2014/01/donor-funding-briefcase-ngos/> (posted 10 December 2013) [accessed 26 September 2016].

Lee, E. (2014) 'Does foreign aid make NGOs corrupt?' in *The Guardian* [online newspaper] <https://www.theguardian.com/global-development-professionals-network/2014/may/01/aid-local-ngos-dishonest-development> (posted 2 May 2014) [accessed on 26 September 2016].

Maxmeister, M. (2017) *Storytelling for change: Story-centered learning for the twenty-first century visionary,* Amazon Digital Services LLC [e-book] <https://www.amazon.com/dp/B01MZ7W1IA/ref=sr_1_4?ie=UTF8&qid=1483971062&sr=8-4&keywords=storytelling+for+change> [accessed 9 January 2017].

Nikolau, L. (2016) 'Pay-it-forward model shows potential for microfinance in developing nations' in *The Humanosphere* [blog] <http://www.humanosphere.org/social-business/2016/04/pay-forward-model-shows-potential-microfinance-developing-nations> (posted 11 April 2016) [accessed 26 September 2016].

Polgreen, L. (2006) 'All the news that fits: Liberia's blackboard headlines' *New York Times* [online newspaper] <http://www.nytimes.com/2006/08/04/world/africa/04liberia.html> (posted 4 August 2006) [accessed 26 September 2016].

Rosenberg, R. (2011) 'Is microcredit over-indebtedness a worldwide problem?' in The Consultative Group to Assist the Poor (CGAP) [blog] <http://www.cgap.org/blog/microcredit-over-indebtedness-worldwide-problem> (posted 7 November 2011) [accessed 26 September 2016].

Schicks, J. (2011) *Over-indebtedness of microborrowers in Ghana: An empirical study from a customer protection perspective,* Center for Financial Inclusion Publication No. 15 [e-book] <https://centerforfinancialinclusionblog.files.wordpress.com/2011/11/111108_cfi_over-indebtedness-in-ghana_jessica-schicks_en_final.pdf> [accessed 26 September 2016].

The 50 Million Missing Campaign (2011) *We Are A Nation of Daughter-Killers, Affirms India's 2011 Census* [website] <http://genderbytes.wordpress.com/2011/04/01/we-are-a-nation-of-daughter-killers-affirms-india%E2%80%99s-2011-census/> (posted 1 April 2011) [accessed 26 September 2016].

Voice of America (2010) 'Liberians literacy awareness' on *In Focus* [news video] <https://www.youtube.com/watch?v=y6_chBRx5Dg> (6 January 2010) [accessed 26 September 2016].

Zaki, J. (2015) 'The feel-good school of philanthropy', *New York Times* [online newspaper] <http://www.nytimes.com/2015/12/06/opinion/sunday/the-feel-good-school-of-philanthropy.html> (posted 5 December 2015) [accessed 26 September 2016].

PART IV
Smart Risk Number 4: Rethinking accountability

Taking smart risks means broadening the way that we evaluate, including seeking feedback directly from those being served, and using a local definition of effectiveness and accountability. Measurement can create a picture of control, or enable leaders to define their own successes.

Keywords: charity rankings; community foundations; humility; effectiveness; financial reports

CHAPTER 18
Charity rankers: Who is defining effectiveness?

Logan Cochrane and Alec Thornton

Let's say your family decides that this holiday, instead of giving each other gifts, you will donate that money to charity. Where should you give? Let's say you are setting up a new foundation. When deciding to support individuals and organizations to address the world's biggest and most complex problems, where does one begin?

With millions of non-governmental organizations working around the world, the process of knowing where to start can be overwhelming. There is a growing list of organizations evaluating registered charities for the purposes of pointing interested donors in the right direction, but even these services and sites can be confusing or misleading.

So many charity rankers

There are over one hundred organizations, groups, and websites seeking to influence donor giving (Mitchell, 2014). Charity ranking organizations influence billions of dollars of donations annually.

A range of ranking systems exist. For example:

- **Charity Navigator** assesses organizations based on their financial health, accountability, and transparency;
- **GiveWell's** grading system adds project types, cost-effectiveness and determines to what extent an organization can benefit from additional funding;
- **Charity Watch** has a grading system;
- **GuideStar** provides financial data about charities and self-reported progress data;
- **Giving What We Can** assesses interventions based on the impact they have on quality of life;
- **Philanthropedia** has an expert-review process;
- **The Life You Can Save** provides a calculator to determine cost effectiveness;
- **GreatNonProfits** has a peer review system; and

http://dx.doi.org/10.3362/9781780449302.018

- **Wise Giving Alliance** provides organizational governance and oversight reports, as well as measures of charity effectiveness.[1]

New technology and tools can empower donors and support the decision-making process to ensure that the values and priorities desired by donors align with their charitable choices. People who work in this field argue that effective giving requires that donors invest time into understanding the issues and organizations, but few donors do so (Ottenhoff and Ulrich, 2012). Deciding which charity ranking recommendations to follow is in and of itself complicated.

Let's take the example of non-profit effectiveness

The notion of non-profit effectiveness is shaped by how it is defined. For example, one donor may wish to achieve the greatest good with a limited amount of funding, focusing upon economic calculations of cost-effectiveness. This may lead them to buy low-cost items, such as mosquito bed nets (discussed below) or deworming pills, and distribute them to the most amount of people possible.[2]

Another donor, however, could define effectiveness in terms of how an intervention or activity obtains equal access for all, meaning the focus is on meeting the basic needs of people who are the most marginalized. Yet another donor could define effectiveness in terms of how sustainable a change is determined to be. This donor may focus on community organizing or advocacy for policy change, which could mean equal access for all in the long term. What we wish to emphasize is the need to understand and critically engage with how non-profits claim their own effectiveness.

Emphasizing cost-effectiveness in terms of cost and impact has drawbacks, particularly when people's preferences have not been considered.[3] A donor may support a charitable organization to provide economic opportunities, but community members may have greater and more urgent priorities, such as the need for clean drinking water.

These are important issues because not all people have equal access to goods and services. In general, those living in remote areas face greater vulnerabilities because of their limited, or lack of, access to services. Communities may not be accessible by roads at all. For example, in the Republic of Congo there are vast disparities in accessing basic healthcare and education services, and these inequalities have not improved significantly over time (International Monetary Fund, 2015). Using only cost-effectiveness to determine how to spend resources in the Congo may prioritize lower cost activities that will reach a greater number of people, i.e. activities will focus on communities that are easier to access.

Development scholar Robert Chambers has called this the 'tarmac and roadside biases', which can 'direct attention towards those who are less poor and away from those who are poorer' (Chambers, 2006). If we view all people as having equal rights to goods and services, then shouldn't we accept that this will be more costly for some people and in some places? If a cost-effectiveness evaluation results in the provision of goods in easier-to-reach communities, the exclusion of others will solidify or increase inequalities.

What if effectiveness was defined by people, not non-profits?

Donors could also consider cases where basic needs are not being met, rather than pre-determining what low-cost products could be distributed to the most people. Rather than providing a good or service that is deemed important by people in places such as Washington, London, or Geneva, the definition of effectiveness could target the priorities of individuals and communities. The result might be clean drinking water instead of deworming treatments, or a transportation service for medical emergencies to the nearest hospital instead of mosquito nets.

A crucial part of establishing an organization's effectiveness is accountability to those whom they ultimately serve – people living in poverty.

Box 18.1 Accountability to whom?

By Jennifer Lentfer

'But how will we hold them accountable?' the senior technical advisor said of the proposal from the high-profile international NGO. 'There's not even a logframe in there.'

Silently, in my cubicle, I thought, 'Oh, *if only* that would only make people and organizations accountable ...'

Obviously, the need and the desire to be accountable in international aid and philanthropy are not going away. With foreign-aid budgets under fire in many donor countries, accountability perhaps becomes even more important.

What I find unfortunate is the automatic associations with accountability. To this senior technical advisor, accountability simply meant the inclusion of a monitoring and evaluation tool known in the aid industry as a logframe, or logical framework, in a proposal to a donor.

There is much to be done to expand the notion of accountability to not only the people giving the money, but most importantly, to the people that social-good organizations serve. This means increasing the appreciation and understanding of accountability beyond risk management and compliance, which often reduces it to abstract concepts or empty exercises.

Demonstrating where the money is going to funders is quite different from representing what percentage of the money actually reaches people.

Can we switch the conversation on accountability to focus on creating concrete, required processes of consultation, transparency, and joint decision-making? Can we acknowledge that when we talk about accountability, we're ultimately talking about power and its role in our aid relationships?

Accountability will never be found on the pages of a proposal or financial report. And if we continue to look only there, we're looking for it in all the wrong places.

Unfortunately, 'customer satisfaction' or 'reviews' are a relatively unexplored and rarely-prioritized aspect of charity rankings. What are people saying about an organization? How dedicated is the staff to the people? Only those on the ground can offer this perspective.

Increasingly, people want to support non-profit organizations that can demonstrate people's involvement and decision-making as a key aspect of successful programming. Not only do they want to see how money was spent, but also how feedback loops informed the projects. Donors must go beyond assuming that needs assessments have been conducted with community members. How will donors know that they were done well and that it was the people who 'owned' the process, not the non-profit? Donors can help widen accountability by asking non-profits to demonstrate how feedback from people participating is incorporated into their work and how it is influencing their approach.

We are not arguing that effectiveness is not important. The question we wish to ask is, 'Effectiveness as defined by whom?'.

Aren't mosquito nets effective?

GiveWell, one of the most influential organizations influencing charitable decision making, ranked an organization distributing long-lasting insecticide-treated nets as its top-rated charity. More than $10 million was given as a result. The evidence for its effectiveness is largely taken from evaluations conducted by other organizations and researchers, working in different countries, even on different continents.

However, the funded organization does not assess if the nets are utilized, used appropriately, shared equally with all members of the family, or if there is any education on the use of such nets when they are distributed.

The calculations that arrived at the decision to support mosquito nets were not based upon an assessment of needs, but on assumptions. The top-ranked charity distributed nets in Malawi, a country where the Global Fund to Fight AIDS, Tuberculosis and Malaria had distributed enough nets for each household, on average, to have three nets (Glassman and Sakuma, 2013). Unlike GiveWell's top-ranked charity, the Global Fund also focuses on long-term impact and is working toward the total elimination of malaria in Malawi. Supply was not the issue. There is plenty of research to suggest consistent usage is not as high as it is assumed (Gamble et al., 2006; Lengeler, 2009). Only 55 per cent of households actually used the nets (Glassman and Sakuma, 2013).

GiveWell did not assess the specific context, the actual impact of this specific organization, or the actual impact of its activities. This calls into question effectiveness based upon the charity ranker's own terms. In addition, GiveWell did not consider human rights or equity, nor did it require projects to conduct thorough needs-assessments, or prioritize the greatest self-identified needs of a community.

Questions charity rankers often can't answer

In reviewing the literature, researchers have attempted to evaluate the differences between charity rankers' methodologies and what measurements are being used to arrive at these recommendations (Lowell, Trelstad, and Meehan, 2005). Human rights and equity are often not assessed in the charity ranking models described above, which is not without consequences. The example above, of prioritizing greatest number reached instead of equal access for all, is one such consequence.

Previous research (Cochrane and Thornton, 2015) has identified limited attention given to a range of unanswered questions, such as:

- Which charities are being evaluated?
- How are they selected?
- Which are not being evaluated?
- How are these decisions made?
- Whose priorities are being taken into account?
- Whose voices matter?
- What other economic and political systems are influencing the impact that charities want to have?
- How can we be sure charities are not exacerbating or perpetuating human rights violations and inequality?
- Are there negative impacts of these simplified charity ranking systems?

Unfortunately, there is not an easy and simple answer when it comes to choosing which charities are best. The problems are complex and require nuanced, context-specific, localized solutions.

Can charity ranking and giving become more contextually-relevant?

Learning from best practices is important, but so is context. What worked in rural Peru may not work in urban Laos. The socio-cultural, political, economic, and historical contexts differ greatly and the uniqueness cannot be ignored (Ramalingam, Miguel, and Primrose, 2014). In the book *One Illness Away: Why People Become Poor and How They Escape Poverty* (2010), Anirudh Krishna argues that too commonly, 'programmes of assistance have followed a pre-determined and broad-brush logic, one that is dictated by people far removed from (and often ignorant about) diverse and changeable local conditions'.

There are platforms that take a different approach to that of the charity rankers, one of the largest of which is GlobalGiving, which is a platform of grassroots projects. The proposed projects are screened after applying.

Although GlobalGiving does not address all the challenges and concerns we have raised, it demonstrates that technology and tools can be used to enable greater participation and engagement for donors, so donors are empowered to make informed choices about their own giving. GlobalGiving (2015) also demonstrates that this can be effective and done at scale, as over $225 million has been donated via its platform by over half a million donors to almost 15,000 projects in 165 countries.

Engaged donors can make informed and effective decisions without the vast simplifications contained in charity rankings, which often use a small selection of evaluated charities and are often based on a range of problematic priorities and generalizations.

Individuals, as a collective, are spending hundreds of millions of dollars. A shift in how that spending occurs can alter the way some of the world's biggest problems are addressed, through funding locally-driven initiatives, projects, organizations, and movements. And individuals are seeking direct engagement with the people needing assistance and building the response based on their needs, rather than an outside formula of effectiveness.

Summary points

- It is difficult for charity rankers to present a whole picture of non-profit work.
- A crucial part of establishing an organization's effectiveness is account-ability to those whom they ultimately serve – people living in poverty.
- Emphasizing cost-effectiveness in terms of cost and impact has drawbacks, particularly when people's preferences have not been considered.

About the authors

Logan Cochrane is a Vanier scholar at the University of British Columbia and a professional development awardee at the International Development Research Centre (IDRC) <https://www.idrc.ca/> in Ottawa, Canada.

Alec Thornton is a senior lecturer in geography at The University of New South Wales, Australia <https://research.unsw.edu.au>.

CHAPTER 19

The solution within: Communities mitigate their own risks

Daniela Gusman

This was not like any other weekly Wednesday meeting. This time, Buhonko, a small village in a mountainous region of eastern Uganda with 54 households, had lost faith in their chairman, Alex.[4] Since he was educated and literate and most of the other village residents were illiterate, the community members had elected Alex as their chairman for a community development project. They became reliant on him, as well as on the primary school head teacher, to write up their project proposal and do the budgets for the project.

Spark MicroGrants facilitates communities in Uganda, Rwanda, and Burundi to compile their own community development plan, to design, implement and sustain projects of their choice by disbursing a small grant of up to $10,000. We had trained community members in Buhonko, and the project collectively chosen by Buhonko community members, which Spark would then fund, was to construct a bridge.

The bridge would help connect their isolated village to another larger town across the river that they visited daily for essential health and education services, as well as to reach the market to sell their produce. The bridge would also save lives, since every year a handful of children die from drowning while crossing the river on foot to get to school. The bridge was going to cost $3,922, of which $3,500 would come from a Spark grant and the balance from community contributions.

After three months of project implementation, work was not progressing. Spark's grant seemed to have been consumed faster than anticipated, despite the budget having been drawn up with the help of the local government district engineer to ensure accuracy. Alex, the chairman, seemed to be holding up the process, not coming to meetings, and showing a decreasing level of commitment.

Community members started to lose faith in him, and began to suspect that he had taken part of the grant for his own personal use. So they asked for a special meeting for the committee to show evidence of where and how the disbursements that had been received from Spark had been spent. However the chairman, who held all the receipts, failed to show up for the meeting. This confirmed their suspicion that he had misused part of the grant.

http://dx.doi.org/10.3362/9781780449302.019

Community members then organized themselves to visit the hardware store where the materials for the bridge had been purchased. They discovered that the chairman had an arrangement where the store was writing higher amounts than the materials cost on the receipts, so that he could pocket the difference.

At this point, as Spark's new Uganda country director, I was tempted to break our grant agreement with Buhonko or at least present the community with an ultimatum – either they reimburse the project with the misused funds immediately, or we void our partnership and pull out from the project altogether.

It was a difficult situation. On one hand, it felt irresponsible to continue to fund a community who had broken our terms of agreement as well as the bond of trust. On the other hand, if we pulled out at this stage it would mean failure for the community, as well as Spark. Our entire approach, our belief in community-driven development as best practice and meeting communities where they are, could be called into question.

When partnering with communities, we spend effort, time, and money on building capability and community responsibility to support the development of collective accountability. This is unlike many organizations that use a disproportionate amount of time and resources analyzing the community's existing capacity to absorb their programmes and funding. Instead, we try to understand if the community is ready for our support – most importantly, whether they have room to grow. We look at a community's commitment and potential to succeed. Initially we gauge this by what proportion of community members come to the meetings and sign the partnership agreement.

The risk we take increases the possibility of communities actually being able to receive a grant and use it well. We prefer this model to due diligence, which, by sheer definition, means investigation of an organization or person, and inherently implies mistrust. Capacity assessments in the traditional sense often put a barrier between the two parties because one has to 'prove' itself to the other. Our ultimate objective is to build independence from aid. At the end of their partnership with Spark, communities are ready to receive funding for their own development plans – ones which they have devised for themselves – not plans that have been imposed by outsiders. They decide whether what an international NGO or donor agency or local government has to offer fits with their priorities.

Thus there were many tough internal discussions between Spark team members, weighing up the importance of sticking to our core values of being facilitators and community-driven, while at the same time adhering to our other core organisational values, of being transparent and honest. So after much deliberation, given our mission, we concluded that it would be best to give the community members some time, let them handle the situation and see what solution they would devise. We agreed upon a timeframe and certain parameters before we would intervene, such as regular updates from the committee members with evidence that they were making headway. We would keep a very close eye on progress and make people in Buhonko aware that they needed to resolve the situation as quickly as possible.

Rather than humiliate Alex by demoting him and publicly accusing him of stealing, community leaders decided on a different strategy, which was a great learning opportunity for the Spark team. We awoke to the canniness, creativity, and democratic thinking of the community members. This is not a strategy that we had thought of and not one that would have necessarily worked out so effectively if it hadn't been the community members who had come up with it.

The committee leaders told Alex that since he was so busy with his work at the primary school and other responsibilities, they would do all his tasks relating to his position as chairman for this project on his behalf. This meant that community members could maintain a good rapport with him. Ultimately they decided that Alex was an invaluable member of the community. He is often called upon to write letters for community members and to advocate for Buhonko with local government officials for the future progress and development of their village.

Alex's responsibilities were then divided and shared between three other committee leaders. Once this happened, the project committee leaders became highly motivated and determined to get the project completed. They did so within four months. They overcame the shortage of funds through increased negotiations on the prices of the remaining items needed to complete the bridge, as well as increasing community contributions.

As a result of this crisis in Buhonko, Spark MicroGrants introduced some more detailed financial training on how community members can reconcile expenditures with receipts. We now also request that at least three community members should be present when making purchases for the project.

In addition, we adopted some new tactics in our grant process, such as making it clear that if savings are made on certain purchases, the total grant amount still remains the same. These savings can be used to purchase additional unforeseen items not on the budget, thus incentivizing community members to negotiate better prices for each item and benefit from these savings.

Since the construction of the bridge has been completed, the lives of the Buhonko residents have been transformed. Belief and confidence in their ability to self-advocate and influence at a local level have been reinstated, since local government fulfilled their promise to join the main road to the village once the bridge had been completed. Committee leaders continue to mobilize the community twice a week to maintain the bridge and connecting roads. In addition there have been improvements in terms of community cohesion and social dynamics. There is a new source of income through the sale of sand from the river bed to nearby villages, which they can now transport over the bridge. The women have also formed a savings and support group, and are building confidence to become leaders in the community.

The story of Buhonko shows how much community members know themselves, that they are best placed to handle their own due diligence and to hold themselves accountable. The community members resolved the conflict, remained united, and are still able to utilize Alex's skills in future. What we learned at Spark MicroGrants is that this can occur without finger-pointing and ruining relationships.

Accountability and trust comes from within and must be a collective responsibility. When exterior entities demand accountability, we do not have a complete picture. When the people on the receiving end of our assistance demand accountability, they are in more control of their futures. Upholding Alex's dignity and trusting the community's own notion of accountability was the best possible lasting and peaceful solution for Buhonko.

Summary points

- Community members are best positioned to hold their leaders accountable.
- When funding at the grassroots level, it can be tempting to cease funding at the first red flag, but tough situations can give way to community-led solutions not seen before.
- Savvy responses to corruption by outsiders can actually build community cohesion.

About the author

Daniela Gusman is co-founder of rise International <http://www.riseint.org>. She was East Africa Director at Spark MicroGrants <http://www.sparkmicrogrants. org> in Uganda from 2013–2016.

CHAPTER 20

Does your financial report make people feel poor?

Nora Lester Murad

When the realization hit me, I went red with shame. We had inflicted the very harm we sought to heal.

We did it with a procedure. A common, bureaucratic requirement: the financial report.

Dalia Association, Palestine's first community foundation, began providing small grants by necessity – we didn't have a lot of money. It was immediately clear, however, that small grants were a critical entry point to support grassroots activists, people who took initiative to work together in groups to improve their communities, without expectation of payment, and without invitation into a formal 'programme'.

Of course, even the grassroots community groups balked at the small grants, ranging from $1,000–$3,000. Palestine is a middle-income country with an economy that is distorted by Israeli occupation and the Oslo Accords. In other words, stuff is expensive. 'What,' they asked with sincere disbelief, 'can we possibly do with only $1,000?'

We set out to prove to people – those who live in remote villages, whose land has been stolen to build the Annexation Wall, whose wells and cisterns are being systematically demolished, whose sons are in prison – that they can meet their own needs with local resources and, in doing so, they can respond to local priorities and not be controlled by foreign agendas. In the course of providing small grants intended to mobilize local resources, my organization sought to value the local resources already available.

Dalia Association's approach to small grantmaking, called 'community-controlled grantmaking' respects Palestinians' rights to self-determination at every step of the process: communities decide which groups will receive grants; they decide how much to allocate to each group; community groups decide how to use the funds without restriction; they say what capacity development they want along with the grant; and communities work together to monitor the grants and decide if and how they were successful.

We didn't realize the financial report could contradict everything we were trying to do.

When time came for the community groups, or grantees, to submit their narrative and financial reports (not only to Dalia Association, but to the entire

http://dx.doi.org/10.3362/9781780449302.020

village in an open, public meeting), we realized we had made a grave mistake. The reports showed how each shekel (approximately 25 cents) had been spent. But where was the grantees' local contribution? The village hall that was used for training sessions, the time of the women who cooked food for participants, the office supplies they got from the municipality, and so much more – none of this was reflected on the financial report. Therefore, these local resources had no apparent value, and we knew this was inaccurate.

The next time Dalia Association did a round of grants, we asked communities to account for their local contributions first during the planning process. We then matched the local contribution dollar for dollar up to the amount of the requested grant.

With this shift in approach, watching grantees build their project budgets was fascinating. In open, transparent, democratic forums, they discussed – perhaps for the first time – how to value their time, their expertise, and their connections. Although our experience shows that increases in external aid often lead to a decrease in volunteerism, our approach motivated grantees to go into the community to ask carpenters and teachers to volunteer, for example. This because for every hour a university student tutored a child in an after school programme, the grantee became vested in money from their grant.

In fact, many funders, large and small, recognize the importance of local contributions. People who invest in their own projects have more incentive to sustain them over the long term. But there is something different and powerful in the way Dalia Association conceptualizes the local contribution. Many funders just ask for a percentage to be listed on the grant application, thus encouraging applicants to inflate their costs to make it appear that they are contributing money they don't actually have. Instead, what I have described is a process that helps people determine the dollar value of what they already give. The village hall, the food cooked for participants, and the office supplies all have a value of which people can be proud. It's a process that consciously seeks to undo damage caused by decades of dependence on international aid. It's a process that helps people re-focus on the value of what they do have rather than on the cash they lack. And it's a process that reminds them that their giving – not external aid – is what keeps their communities going.

In retrospect, there were several unintended consequences to Dalia Association's new approach to accounting. For example, as community groups sought volunteers to work on their small projects, many more people became involved. As a result, the connections and stature of the community groups increased, far in excess of the value of the small grant. They came to be seen, to various extents, as credible community leaders – in the eyes of others, and in their own estimation. Also, grantees were able to think bigger. Rather than plan a $1,000 project, they could plan a $10,000 project and use the cash grant from Dalia Association simply to fill in where local resources weren't flexible enough.

Another unintended consequence was a change in Dalia Association's own procedures. Not only did we change financial reporting for all our grants, but we also were challenged by the grantees to think about our own resources differently. The implications of this new thinking for our community foundation are still unfolding.

Everyone was shocked when the time came to present the financial reports on Dalia Association's small grants to the community. The value of the local community contributions far exceeded the cash grant Dalia Association had provided.

They turned to us, respectfully, and said the words we'd dreamed of hearing: 'We didn't really need your grant. We have the resources to do this work ourselves.' That is the power of a financial report.

Box 20.1 Oral reporting with grassroots organizations – here's why!

By Jennifer Lentfer

The approach of many international grassroots grantmakers is distinguished by their willingness and ability to make application and reporting processes more practical and accessible to grassroots organizations. In effect, they aim to lower the 'glass ceiling' for nascent, indigenous organizations and burgeoning movements to access funding and to decrease the reporting burden on them.

Yet receiving the quality or quantity of written information from grassroots groups that paints a full picture of their work, accomplishments, and challenges can be challenging.

Oral reporting is a way to close this gap. More in-depth and detailed information can be gleaned through a semi-structured interview with grassroots leaders than through only the pages of a poorly-written narrative and financial report. Oral reporting can accommodate any sort of reporting structure/questions/indicators that the partnership requires, though it often still requires a financial report in writing. Perhaps more importantly, it supports the aim of grantmakers to foster open, empowering, and flexible relationships with their grantees.

Objectives of oral reporting

- Decrease the time and effort required from selected grantee partners in preparing a typed, narrative report to donor.
- Enable grantee partners who struggle with written English to more fully describe their work.
- Enhance donor staff's opportunities to appreciate and comprehend the work of grantee partners.

What kinds of grantee organizations can benefit from oral reporting?

- In general – those for whom reporting is a barrier or an undue burden (due to email access, written language usage, etc.).
- Poor reporters – those grantees where you suspect there is more to the story than is coming through on paper.
- Emerging community-based organizations submitting their report for the first time – to help build confidence.
- Fast-moving emerging movements, where formal structures are still being developed or decided upon.
- Organizations where concerns have been noted.
- Organizations with an overdue site visit.

Summary points

- Creating space on the financial report to include community contributions is a way for the community group to show their commitment and their pride in the work. It is a process that helps people re-focus on the value of what they do have rather than on the cash they lack.
- Donors asking after this can help change the dynamic, and help turn around attitudes of dependency.
- With community-controlled grantmaking, communities themselves are responsible for deciding which groups get the funds, how to use the funds without restriction, what capacity development they want along with the grant, and how to determine if and how the grants are successful.

About the author

Nora Lester Murad is a writer and activist in Jerusalem, Palestine. She co-founded Dalia Association <http://www.dalia.ps>, Palestine's community foundation and Aid Watch Palestine <http://www.aidwatch.ps>. She writes about international aid, community philanthropy and life under military occupation at <http://www.noralestermurad.com>.

CHAPTER 21

What 'real-time' community feedback can tell you that evaluations can't

Marc Maxmeister and Joshua Goldstein

I got some alarming emails from a group of youth in Kenya a few years ago. The emails said that a community organization funded by GlobalGiving was exploiting them. The youth claimed that the founder was parading them around when outsiders came by and that he wasn't distributing the goods that had been donated to these kids afterwards.

Eventually, the organization would dissolve. This breakaway group of youth offered the community new leadership under a new organization, causing a widespread shift in attitudes against the founder.

But if that email were to arrive in your inbox, who would you believe? The founder, with whom you had been corresponding for several years? Or the kids' inflammatory accusations?

True community building is neither tidy nor predictable, but is nevertheless possible when feedback facilitates a dialogue. This is the story of how we tried to get to the bottom of this.

The lead-up

The founder 'John' first contacted GlobalGiving to access individual donors through its online fundraising marketplace serving thousands of projects worldwide. Over three years, GlobalGiving facilitated $8,019 in online donations from 193 individuals to a youth sports organization (subsequently referred to as 'Org X') working in a sprawling slum in great need in western Kenya.

With the highest poverty rate (48 per cent) in Kenya, incomes around $40–50 per month (Onim, 2002), HIV/AIDS spreading at epidemic levels, and recovering from the deadly 2007–08 post-election violence, many youth in the area have an overwhelming sense of despair.

Within this challenging environment, and despite limited resources, Org X had been providing opportunities to youth since 2004. Their primary project was a soccer club, operated on the pitch of a nearby school and a community sports stadium. Six days a week, over 150 boys gathered to practice, morning and afternoon. Occasionally, the team was invited to matches both locally and as far away as Kampala, Uganda. Their modest office proudly displayed

http://dx.doi.org/10.3362/9781780449302.021

pictures from tournaments, visits from dignitaries, and certificates from Kenya's Ministry of Youth. Org X also helped an orphanage for children living with HIV/AIDS and a poor rural school.

Over a 14-month period, GlobalGiving facilitated oversight through both a traditional approach, in this case staff visits and a paid professional third-party evaluation, and a more experimental approach involving quarterly self-reports, occasional blog posts from project visitors ('visitor postcards'), impromptu online community feedback, and direct email contact with clients. The following chronicles the findings from each type of oversight.

Staff visits

GlobalGiving sent a staff member to western Kenya in early March 2009 to conduct a workshop on social media for local organizations. Org X volunteered to coordinate this workshop in Kisumu and successfully carried out this task.

Before the workshop, the staff member visited Org X's headquarters. He shared GlobalGiving's work with the founder John and eight youth. He also gave them bumper stickers (like the famous 1-800-How's my driving?) that read, 'What does your community need? Tell us: GlobalGiving.org/ideas'. The staff member emphasized that GlobalGiving wanted to hear directly from the people in the community. No irregularities preceded or prompted this visit, which was part of a series of visits the staff member made to at least six Kenyan organizations during the trip. The staff member did not uncover any irregularities during the brief visit.

Later the same month, GlobalGiving sent another team of visitors to Kenya as part of a programme at George Washington University's master's programme in International Development. Two students met Org X and several youth, and conducted a formal survey they had developed on quantifying project outputs for their final capstone assignment. Several of the 52 survey questions gauged the relationship between organization and the community.

After testing the survey with 20 projects in Kenya, the student surveyors considered these questions essential (Acton et al., 2009) because they provided the best insights into the relationships and the environment surrounding a project, which are two inputs critical for success:

1. Asked of the founder or staff: 'How do you know that you are listening to the beneficiaries and doing what they want?'
2. Asked of a staff member: 'Why did you choose to work for this organization?'

Word-of-mouth feedback

During the students' visit, one youth member of Org X met the students privately and asked the visitor to forward his complaints about the way John was managing the youth sport and education project. The students directed him to submit feedback on the globalgiving.org/ideas website (the one printed on the bumper stickers). His web form response read:

Q: What is your single greatest need?

'How to manage helping orphans, persons living with HIV/aids, promoting the idea of sports to my community, and also making young men in my community understand 'who is god' and what good virtues are needed from them.'

Q: Name one organization that serves you well:

'Formerly it was [Org X] sporting organization but currently the coordinator [John] is evil-minded and corrupt.'

Q: How do you know?

'Because formerly, as I was one of the footballers and an official member, we were being treated with a lot of respect and we also managed to travel to the neighbouring countries for other tournaments; after this things suddenly changed when the coordinator was given Kshs1,000,000 to promote the club, but with his greediness he managed to biologically swallow all the amount to himself and also sold all the balls that were given out.'

This feedback from one disgruntled individual raised concern. A subsequent petition sent by email from another youth confirmed that the first petitioner was not an exceptional case:

> *'I would like you to know that I am one of the [Org X] youths that have been exploited by [John] whereby we decided to call it quits because many organizations have been sending a lot of money and goods to [Org X] yet the evil-minded man is only benefiting himself and his family.*
>
> *Moreover myself and others that have opened their eyes have decided to alert you to come and audit all the amounts that you have been sending to the organization. Also, the Korean Voluntary organization sent him some of the team's items yet he decided to swallow everything by himself. To the rebel members I am a trained HIV/AIDS counsellor so I and others are voluntarily working at our remote villages.'*

This petition included seven other names. Additional interviews revealed that an incident involving a trip to Kampala provided the impetus for youth speaking out through the online form and petition. At the last minute, one group of players had been removed from a team trip for reasons that were never conveyed to them. These youth became angry and, according to an assistant coach, they had threatened to burn down John's house in retaliation and quit Org X.

Instead, the coach urged them to react constructively, and they eventually decided to take their concerns to GlobalGiving via the online form and petition. As one of the youth stated: 'the email was sent because it was the only way to change [John] and still take part in the organization that we like very much.' Interviews also revealed a natural urge amongst recipients to take part in the process of improving their organization. As one youth said,

'We would like to get in contact with the individual donors. If we could get their contacts, youth could be free to email or text them and we can see how we can build the organization.'

The petition was forwarded to a Kenya-based professional evaluator, Leah Ambwaya, whom GlobalGiving had contracted, and who was already scheduled to visit Org X the following month.

Formal evaluation

As part of a planned experiment by GlobalGiving to compare various approaches to gathering information about projects, Leah Ambwaya visited Org X and reported her findings to GlobalGiving and project supporters on 5 May 2009. The two-page evaluation report asks the evaluator to rate and comment on the organization across a wide range of categories ranging from governance to financial status to community engagement.

During her visit, Ambwaya found severe problems with Org X. While she reported an 'overwhelming potential to serve the youth of Kisumu through sports for social change', her report reported serious governance and financial mismanagement issues. She wrote of 'a reluctance to mention the board and how it operates' and a general feeling amongst recipients that John is 'secretary, chairman and board'. Further, 'there were no financial records whatsoever, and the founder himself could not remember how much money he had received from GlobalGiving'. She recommended that the project incorporate the recipients in the decision-making process, and proffer full transparency of all financial records.

Visitor postcards

GlobalGiving arranges site visits for travellers, locals, and any other persons interested in the projects on its online fundraising platform. These visits are designed to verify projects are functioning as described on the website, as well as to produce compelling narratives that will sustain funding for good projects.

In return, visitors submit 'postcards', which are brief third-party observer reports. Akin to a blog post, the visitor postcard is meant to be an informal and personal testimonial of someone who has visited the project. GlobalGiving emails postcards directly to supporters of the project and publishes them on the project page to influence prospective donors.

Visitors to Org X sent three postcards between March and July 2009. On 17 March, GlobalGiving staff (including the co-author of this essay Marc Maxmeister), visited and wrote a postcard. In this excerpt the visitor describes what he saw and how he heard:

> *[Org X's] office was one of the larger shacks on a street in the heart of the slums. It had a nice hand-painted sign. A small crowd of eight youths were gathered there, in preparation for my visit. [John] understands how GlobalGiving works.*

I know because when I talked too fast, he translated into local idioms and heads nodded in recognition of the idea. Here and elsewhere, the Swahili translation for GlobalGiving is 'Harambe'. As one teenager explains: 'when you have something heavy to lift and you cannot do it yourself, you yell "harambe" and the people come help you so everyone does it together'. Harambe is a village revival fundraising event where the people pool their money to support a common purpose. [John] said, 'GlobalGiving is Harambe for our sport project on the internet'.

We handed out bumper stickers that say, 'What does your community need?' and the site: www.globalgiving.org/ideas. They were a hit. Everyone likes stickers, even if they don't quite understand the website part. We're trying to engage kids in slums like Minyata to tell us (and you) what they need most.

A few weeks later on 21 April, two members of the student survey team sent a postcard, excerpted below:

Kara: *It was a busy day, spent visiting the office, the staff, and two schools in Kisumu and the surrounding areas. Although [Org X's] main initiative seems to be focused on combining sports and education, it has also worked with women who fled to Kisumu after the post-election violence in 2008. I saw the sadness on their faces and in their words as they described losing husbands and homes in the violence. However, I am not exactly sure what [Org X] is doing for these women ...*

A few things surprised me during our visit. 1) We were supposed to visit the orphanage that is run by [Org X], but we never got the chance, which surprised me since their main project on GlobalGiving has to do with those orphans. 2) [John] asked us for a lot of money throughout the day: to rent an expensive car, to pay for footballs and snacks for the school kids, to buy benches for the schools, to get him a digital camera, to tip the driver, to buy drinks for the football team, and more. By the end of the day, I literally had no money in my pockets, and I left feeling a bit taken advantage of, a feeling I did not have at any of the other organizations we visited. 3) I was surprised by the focus on serving just the Luo tribe and the animosity of the staff toward other tribes.

Christine: *We started off the visit by seeing his office, a one-room space open to the street. I met with the volunteers that help [Org X], and heard about how great their soccer team was. The team seemed to be a major focus for the volunteers, and I learned a little about what they do for the community ...*

Throughout the day, [John] repeatedly asked me and my partner to purchase things for the soccer team and the children. It was clear that providing for so many beneficiaries weighs heavily on him, especially considering how diverse his constituency is. It's a shame because I do believe that [Org X] is doing good work, but their approach is a turn-off. Only hearing about the need, but never about the work being done doesn't encourage support.

One month later, when the evaluator Leah Ambwaya visited, she wrote an illuminating report that GlobalGiving sent to donors on 14 May as a postcard and part of the larger formal evaluation. She quotes a project participant

---

Box 21.1 Transparency and nuance: A funder's perspective

As these events surrounding Org X transpired, the postcards, the full evaluator's report, and Org X's narrative summary appeared on the GlobalGiving website. One donor comment on this report captured the nuances of implementing work under the difficult circumstances:

I think it's hard to run any organization, but with that said, non-profits need to be clear with the donor community and the recipients about their goals and progress. [Org X] is not clear about how funds are spent and even [John's] update reports to GlobalGiving raised red flags with me. There are too many other good projects out there; I will support those.

---

named Mwangi.[5] Mwangi stressed Org X's successes at giving youth positive alternatives to drugs and idleness, while also addressing the ways that the organization failed to meet the needs of the community:

We talked to Mwangi, a 16-year-old orphan who dropped out of school in Form four due to lack of school fees. We sought his permission to record this discussion on tape, to which he consented.

I quote: 'My name is Mwangi. I started playing for [this organization] in 2008; I play full back. I dropped out of school this year due to lack of school fees; I was in Form four. I do not have any hope of going back to school since my two elder brothers are unemployed and cannot help at all. I come for practice twice a day (morning and evening).

This project keeps me busy and also keeps me away from getting myself into a lot of trouble like doing drugs and other antisocial things that many young people get into due to desperation. I don't even know if I will ever go back to school, the chances are very minimal.

Mwangi continued:

We don't even go to the office or help out with any work at the office. As much as we have been offered the opportunity to join the team, we also have our own challenges with the club, but we are not given a chance to express ourselves. If you do, then you are kicked out of the club. This project can help the youth more, if we can be given some roles to play.

'Does the director listen to you?' Ambwaya continued. 'You can't dare speak, you will be kicked out.' However, Mwangi affirms that some of them had travelled to Tanzania for a tournament some time last year.

When Ambwaya asked Mwangi and his fellow petitioners whether Org X should continue receiving donations through GlobalGiving during her visit, they replied 'yes' at that time, but asked for more oversight.

Volunteer support and a turning point

Earlier in 2009, we learned that John had requested help from a conflict-resolution master's degree programme at the University of Oregon. Partly because of the visibility of this ongoing dialogue on the GlobalGiving website, a conflict-resolution professor, Hicks, arranged for two conflict-resolution students to intern with Org X in the summer. The professor visited Org X for nine days and worked with John to arrange and document what the student interns would do and what Org X had committed to.

The two key areas they planned to address were organizational development, particularly moving towards more transparent financial management, and improved internal communication and conflict-resolution. The professor sent his impressions to donors as a visitor postcard in May of 2009, excerpted here:

> *All in all, this is very much a legitimate organization doing good work and worth supporting. Over the next six months, I believe it will develop the organizational management systems that will increase transparency and accountability. I believe that there is tremendous potential for [Org X] to make even more of a difference for orphaned youth, widows, and the community at large.*

The student interns attempted to work with youth and staff at improving Org X for several months (June to August 2009). Their experience confirmed earlier reports that there was widespread frustration among the youth. They organized meetings to foster understanding and facilitated closer ties between Org X and another youth sports organization working in the same region.

The interns were impressed by the inclusive way the peer organization listened to and empowered its youth through sports. The interns reported that this increased their resolve to seek improvement at Org X. Ultimately, the interns were frustrated in their efforts by the lack of commitment from John. One intern wrote:

> *[John] says the right things in meetings and then immediately begins to operate on his own terms when he leaves. We also began meeting with many more community members, some of whom were former members of Org X. We heard many stories about how poorly he has treated his members and many accusations of thievery. I am not saying I believe all of these stories but it also became clear that the conflict was escalating and that I needed to figure something out ... After discussions with [several youth] involved with [Org X] the decision was made to start a new organization that would successfully address the problems in [the community].*

Up until this point, all stakeholders shared the view that organization was bringing more good to the community than would otherwise be possible without it. When asked, 'Should this organization continue to fundraise on GlobalGiving?', every visitor and youth affected answered yes.

That was until two community leaders in Kisumu decided to create a splinter organization to parallel Org X's work in the community. At the moment when youth had a choice between two alternatives, i.e. remaining with the organization or joining a new youth-led initiative, the majority of them withdrew support for Org X. The conflict-resolution students also decided to devote their energy to helping the new organization.

In the subsequent weeks, other community members followed suit. The principal of a local school revoked Org X's right to use the practice fields, citing the founder's long-standing failure to deliver on promises to provide support for upkeep of the grounds. With Org X expelled and isolated, John left the community altogether after many years of service. John continued to try to promote his organization, although he appears to be the sole member.

What now? A mobile survey

There had been underlying signs that the youth were not fully satisfied all along. When we initially posed the question, 'Should this organization continue to receive donations through GlobalGiving?' the youth, project visitors, a formal evaluator, and the donors all agreed that the it should continue despite the struggles reported on the ground. All asked that GlobalGiving continue to work cooperatively with the organization and suggested tangible goals for improvement.

But now things had changed. It was obvious that the community wanted to be served by a different organization. With this continual feedback loop occurring through various sources, GlobalGiving could now pinpoint the moment when all stakeholders' attitudes towards John and Org X changed.

This clarity allowed us to take immediate action: to conduct a final informal phone and SMS survey of community members to: (a) confirm that they now supported removing Org X; and (b) to let them know their feedback initiated this action, explained within the context of lessons learned. We again asked, 'Should this organization be removed from GlobalGiving?'

Over 40 youth, other community members, and the interns who had recently worked with Org X said that it should be removed. Even a community member working at another funding agency wanted us to remove it, and cited our feedback efforts as a reason why he too was no longer supporting them, but now favoured the new splinter organization. Three eyewitnesses reported that Org X's offices were closed, including a neutral community member who had no prior relationship with Org X or its youth. When presented with clear evidence of a change in attitudes from the community, we did not hesitate to remove this organization. Although the people and John couldn't resolve their differences, we had helped everyone be heard.

Why feedback loops matter

Although the long-term impact of creating stronger feedback loops in Org X's community will not be known for years to come, the feedback that was received over this six-month period allowed the events and interventions described here to more accurately reflect the desires of the community served. Org X's story illustrates the essential value of a real-time feedback loop: sustaining dialogues that continuously draw attention to a project's environment, with an emphasis on the cooperation necessary for positive community impact.

Conversely, this narrative underscores the power of feedback to accelerate social change when leadership resists the will of the community it serves. Without a deliberate effort to promote dialogue, the underlying problems in this community might have taken years to resolve and could have erupted in deep conflict, as had happened throughout the region just 18 months before.

Building feedback-loop approaches may be uniquely valuable for the oversight of community development in four ways. First, this approach allows more participation through more channels, particularly the most interested parties. Second, this approach generates signals that force others to take action to resolve the underlying problems faster. Seeing negative visitor feedback appear on a webpage just days after a visit caused John much consternation, leading to immediate action that was constructive, at first. Third, direct feedback circumvents the principal/agent problem inherent in international aid and philanthropy, where Org X's funders (principal) have trouble communicating with recipients (another principal) because of their dependence on implementers and evaluators such as John, GlobalGiving staff, and Leah Ambwaya (agents). Finally, feedback loops enable leaders to embrace a mindset of fruitful failure, or an acceptance of the experimentation and flexibility that enables quick adjustments to be made.

How feedback differs from evaluation

Traditional monitoring and evaluation has always been expensive, slow, required, and flawed – but monitoring and evaluation based on community feedback is fast, cheap, and effective – and it requires us to think about how we work in a different way.

Despite the insightful commentary from the professional evaluator in this case, her perception was necessarily shaped by a few choice interviews; the bulk of the community was not included in her evaluation. Similarly, power relationships impair the ability of staff to gather direct feedback, as evidenced by the absence of warning flags in the postcard sent by the first staff member to visit Org X. A better approach is to educate communities on how to submit real-time feedback through tools that protect individuals from retribution.

Providing an SMS-based feedback system or passing out bumper stickers with the website address, and subsidizing the small (yet significant) amount of money required to visit an internet café are great investments compared to the hourly wage of professional evaluators. And, even in the best cases, formal evaluations relay information about community needs through intermediaries. Feedback tools provide evaluators with more leads for follow-up interviews.

As a final reflection on feedback loops, the discrepancy between Org X's outward prosperity and the poor relationship it had with the youth it aimed to serve highlights a serious limitation to the formal evaluation.

This organization had been operating for over five years, attracted regional and international funding from many sources, and claimed to have 2 staff, 22 volunteers, and 640 members. The standard action for most funders upon recognizing irregularities would be to abandon Org X, because the risks outweigh the potential impact.

People are the experts on whether they are being well-served by a development project or organization. Our formal evaluation stressed low community involvement as a critical problem, but the evaluation process could not fix this problem. In contrast, monitoring through a continuous feedback loop forces stakeholders to join together in finding a workable solution, because the people raising concerns are also the ones most likely to improve the environment. The feedback-loop approach facilitates solutions, rather than merely identifying problems.

Elements and tools of feedback loops

So what, in particular, separates the feedback-centred, distributed decision-making process from traditional, formal evaluations? We note three elements: crowdsourcing; creation of an enabling environment; and new technology.

Crowdsourcing

Whereas the unit of information in the formal evaluation is one complete self-contained report, feedback loops generate information fragments that must be filtered and aggregated; a task best performed through crowdsourcing to both advocates and everyday participants and observers of a project.

Technology-aided feedback loops put the audience in control of the messages with a similar dynamic to that of social media. Each member is encouraged to consume content from others, but also to adopt and alter the message as it spreads through informal networks. Conversations are the unit of communication, not monologues. The efficiency of the message is dictated by the tendency of each person to pass it on to friends. Therefore the messages must be interesting, rewarding, and/or important. This collaborative filtering of project and personal information disseminates the most important information to the widest audience automatically.

Creation of an enabling environment

While the traditional evaluation relies mostly on human visits and report-writing, information in feedback loops is predominantly relayed through mobile phones and the internet in a rapid-fire, conversational manner that triggers immediate responses. For messages from the community to bubble up and influence the direction of projects, mechanisms for evaluation must also follow the guidelines of social media to work. Whereas most formal evaluation frameworks focus on quantifying results and predicting future impact, a continuous-feedback dynamics approach tries to create an enabling environment.

Conversations surrounding the project provide the raw material for leaders to draw insights on how better to achieve goals, from the community's perspective. If the environment surrounding a community project is fraught with conflict, the project itself will not succeed and persist. Likewise, the absence of feedback from citizens can signify a lack of community involvement. Thus sustaining and monitoring conversations among stakeholders surrounding the project can be an effective means of achieving higher-impact results.

Technology

Until recently, garnering informal feedback from participants in projects halfway across the world was simply unfeasible. With the rise of web and mobile networks over the last decade, however, real-time feedback and meaningful communication between donors and recipients is now possible. Yochai Benkler (2006) describes this new reality as the 'networked public sphere', an information environment characterized by many-to-many communication (instead of just one-to-many or one-to-one) at near-zero cost. WhatsApp and Facebook Zero are examples of popular phone-based social networks. Unlike the industrialized world, the networked public sphere in the developing world exists primarily through mobile phones. The following technologies are essential for enabling feedback from communities:

SMS-based social networks The vanguard of these systems is currently FrontlineSMS, a service that allows organizations to send one-to-many and many-to-many text messages within a region. Only one laptop is required, so long as group members have a mobile signal. Given that an estimated four billion people had cell phones in 2009 (International Telecommunications Union, 2009), and there were over 500 million cell phones in Africa alone, the reach of SMS-based social networks likely covers the majority of villages on earth (assuming many people still without mobile phones have access through a friend or relative).

This tool has been tested by dozens of NGO leaders, clinics and political activists throughout the developing world who use it to reach their staff or constituencies. Specifically, Zimbabweans report human rights abuses, Indonesian commodity markets send prices to farmers, and Nigerian election monitors reported election irregularities. Messages can be aggregated for surveys or forwarded to websites (SMS-to-web).

Other networks with more functionality are quickly becoming available throughout the developing world. The most prominent of these networks is MXit, a South African mobile social network with over 14 million users that allows profile-building, friending and other functionality. In Uganda, a product called status.ug is enabling users without smart phones to update global networks like Facebook via SMS, and take part in a mobile marketplace. In each of these instances, organizations are creating feedback loops that allow them to request and report information more quickly, catch problems before they escalate, and encourage members to take a more active role in their organization.

Mobile money While social networks enable information to be shared in feedback loops, mobile money services will be necessary to reimburse village-level 'micro-evaluators' and for promoting the more widespread adoption of feedback tools. Throughout the developing world, network providers are increasingly launching mobile money-transfer services that allow users to deposit money with agents anywhere in the country, and then send money to friends and family via mobile phone. The most well-known of these services, M-Pesa, a service of Kenyan network provider Safaricom, had over five million users and transferred over $1 billion in 2008 (IT News, 2009). The most popular use is to send money from the commercial centres to families in villages. Increasingly, these services are being used to pay for services and for employee wages.

Conclusion

Org X's story provides a snapshot of what feedback loops can do when ongoing funding is triggered or withheld based on the real-time information from grateful or underserved community clients. It illustrates that dynamic feedback between everyday citizens, non-profits, and the donor community brings together the forces for change.

Rapidly spreading new technologies, particularly mobile phones and SMS-to-web interfaces (e.g. Twitter), now allow villagers to report continuously on project progress, and ultimately to guide non-profits, if given proper incentives. These technology-aided feedback loops will enable clients to guide practitioners throughout project or programme implementation, share real-time information, and drive donors during the funding process.

Poor communications between non-profits and the communities they serve can lead to wasted resources (in mild cases) or the threat of outright violence (in serious cases), and can dramatically undermine the results of their efforts. Moving towards a system that emphasizes feedback and communication allows the community and social-good organizations to work together and move in new directions. The upheaval that results from dialogue could be a necessary step for the community to move forward, causing new efforts, movements, and institutions to continuously emerge.

Social change is neither tidy nor linear, but more a flexible approach to evaluation, such as continuous feedback loops, – can be used to manage the present environment and thus enable deeper future impact.

Summary points

- Without a deliberate effort to promote dialogue and seek feedback, the underlying problems in a community might take years to resolve.
- Feedback differs from evaluation because people are experts, not outsiders. While the traditional evaluation relies mostly on human visits and report writing, SMS-text technology can enable feedback directly from those being served by community organizations.
- Feedback loops can be created through mobile phones and the internet in a rapid-fire, conversational manner that triggers immediate responses.

About the authors

Marc Maxmeister is chief innovation officer at Keystone Accountability <http://keystoneaccountability.org> in Washington, DC. He created and managed GlobalGiving's <https://www.globalgiving.org> Storytelling Project from 2009 to 2015 and from it built the data analysis tools at storylearning. org <http://storylearning.org/>.

Joshua Goldstein is CEO of The Department of Better Technology, Inc <https://www.dobt.co>. He has worked for the World Bank Group, Google and UNICEF Innovations, helped launch Code4Kenya, and co-founded Apps4Africa.

CHAPTER 22
Dusty sneakers, girls' dorms, and challenging our assumptions

Sasha Rabsey

The red dust is still in the fabric of my sneakers. I've been home from Burkina Faso for a week. I can still remember being led by village women through dusty millet fields to their wonderful new grain mill, its mortar still fresh.

Burkina Faso is a West African nation that appears annually on the list of three of the poorest countries on earth. I had gone to visit a grantee of my foundation, the HOW Fund. For three years I had been supporting Aminata Diallo, who works with teenage girls around issues of sexual reproductive rights, family planning, female genital cutting, education, and job skills.

I don't want to shake out the dust in my shoes, because the day I spent with Aminata and the women of Yirwal, a small village near Bama, was the day I discovered the power of grassroots grantmaking and the humility needed to accompany it. That day, and the discussions and reflections that followed over the next five days, completely reshaped my thinking about my work.

Many donors begin their work with set criteria a grantee must satisfy. Does the project have impact? Can it go to scale? Will 'behaviour change' be lasting? Before visiting Aminata, I had had an increasingly uneasy relationship to these concepts, and thought often about my own criteria for funding – how much do my decisions depend on my head, how much on intuition, how much on heart? In particular, to me, the 'thou shalt go to scale' command in the social innovation world sometimes sounds as inflexible and prescriptive as a parent shaking a finger at a naughty child.

Aminata is a quiet, fine-boned high-school philosophy teacher with a fierce loyalty and unyielding commitment to keeping young girls in school. Tired of watching teenaged girls become pregnant and then marginalized year after year, Aminata took action. She founded her organization, Maia, and began her work by creating 'listening posts' where girls could have confidential conversations around issues of sexuality and family planning.

This may sound like a simplistic innovation, but a domino effect soon took hold. The listening posts quickly turned into mother's clubs, vocational training, teacher training, a preschool, a rural women's initiative ... the list goes on. From Aminata's simple idea came an interconnected network of impactful community projects. My small, three-year unrestricted grant gave

http://dx.doi.org/10.3362/9781780449302.022

Aminata the support she needed to take a sabbatical from her job and devote herself full-time to her work, giving it traction, stability and depth.

Just one of the many initiatives Maia has fostered illuminates why I view Aminata's work as impactful and systems-changing: the building of a girls dormitory. At a middle school in a remote village near Yirwal, an unprecedented thirty girls became pregnant during a single school year. Subsequently, all of the girls left school permanently due to the stigma of being an unwed mother. Aminata could have tackled the problem conventionally, by going into the school and lecturing on the evils of premarital sex and teen pregnancy. But that would have been pointless since she reported that many of these girls didn't even know how they became pregnant, as it was not common practice for mothers to discuss sexuality with their daughters. Instead of lectures and training, Aminata garnered community support and built a girl's dormitory.

Why a dormitory? Because she saw that the girls from the surrounding villages had to travel nearly four miles each way to get to school. This left them vulnerable. In order to decrease travel time, many girls stayed in the homes of relatives, friends, or acquaintances in closer proximity to the school. Without parental supervision and a lack of even a rudimentary knowledge of sex, the girls were often preyed upon by men and boys in their host homes or by teachers or staff at school. Girls making the long walk every day might be interrupted by someone along the path or stopped by someone in a neighbouring village where they were casually coerced into sex or raped.

Aminata had already aligned with the community over the desire to keep girls safe and in school. She had developed a curriculum focused on sexuality and family planning for the middle school. But the dormitory was the real game changer. Five days a week, eighteen girls live in a small cement structure surrounded by a fence with a metal gate. There are two rooms with colourful straw mats on the floor where the girls sleep, study, and are safe to act like adolescent girls. A couple from the community, Isa and Awa, are the trusted dorm parents and their job is to care for the girls.

Box 22.1 The problem with pity

By Jennifer Lentfer

Pity emphasizes people's perceived weaknesses, making us feel better about ourselves.

It can make others the victims and ourselves the heroes.

It is insidious. It can fuel 'us' vs. 'them'.

But there is no such thing as us and them, actually.

People don't want pity or charity. They want opportunities, and solidarity, and hope.

How we see the people we attempt to help affects how we act towards them.

Thus, social change begins with seeing others, and ourselves, as fully human.

Soon a mother's group grew out of the communal desire to support the girls' efforts to stay in school. Each mother took her turn cooking and carrying pots of food the four miles to the dormitory. All eighteen of the original girls have now graduated and are planning to advance to high school, an extraordinary statistic in the village.

Perhaps the most striking evidence of impact is that there is now community pressure on parents to support their girls' efforts at educational advancement. No longer do they want to be the parents who thwart their child's ambitions by pulling them out of school in order to help at home or to be married off. So, as a result of Aminata's simple innovation, not only do girls have a newly acquired status in the community, so do the parents!

The key to Aminata's success, though, has been her ability to build an alliance with community members and other stakeholders based on trust and cooperation, an alliance that addresses a community problem with a community-based initiative. This trust-building is in contrast to projects and solutions that are dropped in from the outside with a clear mandate but without buy-in from the community. The impact of Aminata's work is far reaching: ultimately what she has created will open the way for social transformation in village after village.

What did I learn in Yirwal? For five years, I had been checking grantees for healthy financials and then using my gut instinct about the grantee and the work to make funding decisions. So far this has worked for me. My intuition presents a road map. Any other donor could easily quantify parts of what I saw, but what I experienced in Yirwal demonstrated just how right Aminata's bottom-up grassroots approach really was in three ways.

First, Aminata taught me to check my arrogance and my assumptions. The conclusion of 'rightness' is personal. The first – and maybe the worst – assumption that I can make is that as an educated, resource-endowed person with a desire to help, I have valuable opinions and advice to offer. Aminata showed me that the exact opposite was true. The best thing I did was to provide the grant to Aminata, then step aside – listen, watch, and learn.

Aminata also taught me to ease up on rigid criteria and definable outputs. There are so many outcomes that you cannot quantifiably measure, but that are no less valuable and relevant. Over time I have seen that unintended outcomes are often more important than the quantitative data I see in a report. I prefer a nuanced picture and continual reflection on the far-reaching outcomes of programmes and community organizing over time.

Finally, a great idea cannot be implemented by just anyone. When you are talking about changing long-held attitudes, finding leaders with the trust and knowledge of the community is key. Lasting change most often starts with just one person and the family and community around them.

A dormitory for eighteen girls may not sound like much, but for those girls, it was everything.

Summary points

- Outsiders can rarely fully understand local culture and national systems.
- Funders often rely on rigid criteria and definable outputs. Many outcomes that cannot be quantifiably measured are no less valuable and relevant.
- Realize you are backing people as well as ideas. A great idea cannot be implemented by just anyone.

About the author

Sasha Rabsey is founder of the HOW Fund <http://www.howfund.org> in California, USA.

CHAPTER 23

Rigorous humility: Reconciling the desire for certainty and the space for possibility[6]

Jennifer Lentfer

It was seemingly straightforward. We provided a small grant to an income-generating project in Malawi. It was to a youthful and energetic group that wanted to start a chicken project, and sell the eggs and the offspring to generate revenue to support their work with children and families. But in their first grant report to us, the group explained that they had not seen any profit. That was, you see, because a 'beast' had eaten all of the chickens.

This is also why the group wanted to now abandon chicken-rearing in favour of installing a paraffin pump, much like a gas (petrol) pump though this one would sell oil to light people's homes and provide fuel for cooking. According to the group in Malawi, this change in strategy away from the chickens would require much less maintenance and security once it was up and running.

I was faced with a question – would I fund this group again? What would it take for you to do so? More information? A little faith? Or a lot, for that matter?

To try to make an impact in the world means our work is often focused on unanswered questions. What is development? What is social change? What is aid, philanthropy, social enterprise, impact investing? Do they necessarily improve the lives of people who are poor? How can outsiders help in the most effective and sustainable ways? How do we best support local leaders and grassroots organizations as strong forces for change in their communities? What kinds of beasts live in Malawi and how *does* one get into the chicken coop?

Many of us have observed what some call the growing 'data dash' of recent years in the government, international aid, and philanthropic sectors. In an annual letter from his foundation, Bill Gates (2013) gave us the gospel of measuring what we do. As a grantmaker, and as a monitoring and evaluation professional, I have personally been a part of an increasing effort by donors and non-profits to find more precise ways of measuring progress in order to make consequential judgments. I've heard these phrases, over and over, in myriad ways and contexts:

> *It's vital that we understand what works and what doesn't work and why.*
> *That's all very well and good, but how would you measure that?*
> *And when do you anticipate that you'll be able to see the results from this?*

http://dx.doi.org/10.3362/9781780449302.023

In fact, the search for evidence has become ingrained in every aspect of grantmakers' and grantseekers' day-to-day work. Obviously, no one wants to see resources squandered and so it's natural to look for ways to prevent this. Some people see evidence-seeking behaviour in a very positive light. To them, social-change work will be more effective and less wasteful of resources if it is guided by data and objective decisions. The logic goes that with more information at our fingertips, we can take stronger steps towards ensuring accountability and value for money. Without measuring our progress, what we are doing is useless.

Some people see the search for evidence in a different light – as onerous, limiting, tedious, time-consuming, burdensome, and expensive. They see social change as a force beyond logic and induction. I've worked extensively in building the monitoring and evaluation capacity of grassroots organizations in Africa. What I have found is that abstract metrics and big data often don't often help people understand their relationship to improving the well-being of those around them. Rather local leaders, as members of a community, read real-time trends via observation of what's happening on the ground. To local leaders, research design is often quite far from the difficult, intimate, or complex factors at play in the real work of social change. Grassroots groups, not just donors, need ways to learn and evaluate their work that make sense for them.

It is worth exploring the differing worldviews of the thinkers (or the people who make decisions behind their desks, based on the information before them) and the doers (or those working on the ground, with communities, families, and individuals in their change processes). Are these irreconcilable worldviews? Do you see the value in the rising demand for evidence? Or do you identify more with those who need resources to carry out their work? What happens as funders gain a bigger and bigger appetite for evidence?

There is absolutely nothing wrong with deepening the thinking behind the doing. My own career has been devoted to this very endeavour. The labels I have used, 'thinkers' and 'doers', are completely artificial. Though many of us will find ourselves more readily identifying with one camp than the other, we definitely need more thinking doers and more doing thinkers. What's needed for us all to listen more effectively and become more responsive to those at the forefront of social transformation? Can we as grantmakers acknowledge and challenge our own policies and practices that can often marginalize and demotivate local leaders? Are we looking for accountability only on the pages of a proposal or financial report?

Firstly, we need to consider the dangers of an increasing desperation to solve the world's problems using rigorous measurement. Why have quantitative and generalizable information, randomized control trials, become the gold standard by which social change work can be measured? Have we even asked ourselves enough *why* we are doing all this measuring?

Pssst ... because here's the deal. The reasons we're doing all this measuring is not only about obtaining information to feed our rational thinking minds.

It's about fear, pure and simple. We're afraid we don't have enough information. We're afraid to make a bad decision. Why do we need to address the fear head on? Because I have witnessed that the space for possibility shrinks when a person's or an organization's need for certainty or control takes over.

The consequences of fear

There are very real consequences of this to consider when it comes to our social-change work, consequences for our partners and, most importantly, for ourselves.

For those working with communities

Searching for evidence in practice can mean imposing funders' needs on people who are in the process of organizing at local levels. This can be a severe drain on their already-scarce time and resources. Funders' risk-aversion can constrain local leaders' decision-making and responsiveness to communities. Their fear can limit possibilities or the ability to even see possibilities.

Because of the power imbalances inherent in funding relationships, funders can easily distract partners from their mission and constituencies. Do funders adequately consider and analyse the real costs of time and resources devoted to overly-complicated reporting, evaluation, or research exercises? Are funders offering useful capital if our lengthy proposals, burdensome reporting, and heavy-handed funding mechanisms get in the way of people doing the social-change work they've set out to do?

For funding relationships

A former administrator of the United Stated Agency for International Development (USAID), Andrew Natsios (2010), coined the term 'obsessive measurement disorder' to refer to the rules and reporting requirements that crowd out creative work and create the wrong kind of incentives in the inter-national aid sector. Natios argues that obsessive measurement disorder stifles innovation and leads to a focus on short-term results.

Natios is asking: Where's the room for possibility and innovation if we're always looking for what's wrong? From my own experience in the inter-national aid and philanthropy sector, I can tell you that data-gathering or reporting solely for the purpose of accountability to funders fails time and again to result in improvements at the community level.

Obsessive measurement disorder can deepen the inequalities in funding relationships, leading to a lack of trust and understanding between the thinkers and the doers. I have observed that often the search for evidence creates a glass ceiling to prevent the involvement of those who supposedly matter most – those whose lives we are hoping to affect. An over-reliance on generalizable data especially leaves those without a graduate degree behind.

However brilliant the indicators or survey questions, thinkers and doers should both be concerned that obsessive measurement disorder may actually be hurting our decision-making processes.

For ourselves

No matter how self-aware we are when we begin work in social change, many people will be operating from a worldview in which change in poor or marginalized people's lives is only possible with our help. We may believe that change will occur with enough hard work, sound management, and commitment.

After almost 15 years of doing social-change work, the jury is still out on this in my mind. In my career, I have found that the international aid and philanthropy sector tends to be overly technocratic and detached. Because most people are working from their desks in capital cities, ordinary people's lives are often just a concept or an abstraction. When I started, my young, idealistic self was driven by passion. Even if naïve, I was excited about the possibility of making the world better. I suspect that all of you reading this started in that very same place.

I meet every year with a group of impressive young people from an organization called Thinking Beyond Borders. They come having just returned from a gap year, travelling to four countries where they focus on studying development theory and learning how to become effective agents of change. They spend their first week back in the US in Washington DC to meet with various multilateral agencies and international NGOs. Here's what one of the students wrote to me in their thank-you note afterwards: 'After a week of some somewhat disheartening meetings, it was great to see that somebody in this town has a pulse!'

These young people were so hungry, after only a week among international development professionals, for an open and real conversation about social change! Their new eyes reminded me about how much abstract ways of thinking frame this work. Obsessive measurement disorder is a symptom of this.

We can appear less sensitive, hardened, more disconnected, less caring, less open to possibility – qualities that do not make for good partnerships. Our ability as thinkers to high-mindedly question everything about 'what works' can insulate us. It can become a tool of our egos and create a 'gotcha' mentality. And it can remove us far from the realities of ordinary people.

What is rigorous humility and how can it help face our fears?

An idea I call *rigorous humility* can help us prevent and mitigate an unhealthy fixation on evidence and measurement. It can also help us to listen more effectively. We can use rigorous humility to remain unsatisfied with disappointing results, and yet begin to embrace the mystery of how social change occurs.

As humans, we are drawn to explore, examine, and respond to the world around us. Not surprisingly, then, the concept of rigorous humility has its roots in all faith traditions and is also a key part of the scientific process. It is found in the searching for answers in which we are continually engaged.

Gandhi (1993) explains it this way:

> *The instruments for the quest of truth are as simple as they are difficult. They may appear quite impossible to an arrogant person, and quite possible to an innocent child. The seeker after truth should be humbler than the dust … Only then, and not until then, will he have a glimpse of the truth.*

The most effective and inspiring community leaders, philanthropists, social entrepreneurs, development practitioners, and agents of change I've ever worked with embody rigorous humility. They know the limits of their experience and their attitude and actions reflect that they see themselves as only one of *many*. Rigorous humility involves:

- Giving up the role of expert.
- Concrete steps to bring power imbalances into check.
- Active engagement in self-reflection.
- Most importantly, seeing others' full potential to be capable agents of change, *with or without us.*

Three things differentiate a person who is rigorously humble. First, a way to tell if a person is using rigorous humility is to listen carefully when they speak. You are listening for *one key phrase:* 'I don't know'.

Using 'I don't know' as an acceptable answer to a question requires something different of us. We must step away from the usual role or position of authority, or people who know or are 'in the know'. Most of us are unconsciously trying to avoid critique and the judgment of our peers. This happens as a result of our education and training, organizational processes, and our own fears. We don't want to appear foolish, or indecisive. Why? Because that is a very vulnerable place to be. Indeed, 'I don't know' is a very vulnerable place to be.

But that is not necessarily a bad thing. A commenter, on my blog how-matters.org (2011) once explained it like this:

> *We have to start somewhere, usually with paradigms taught in institutions that we must reforge into our own usable tools, honed and tempered though trial, tribulation, and error. By difficult challenges not overcome, we come to the ego-deflating realization that 'I do not know enough' and then, 'I can never know enough.' And we cry. We are soothed by those that say, 'What can we do but keep on trying?' And so we keep on learning and applying through experience and perseverance what we had wished we had known, comforted by the knowledge that if we had waited until we knew what we needed to know, we would never have made it.*

This cycle is rigorous humility. 'I don't know' is found in imprecise information, in unseen or undetectable outcomes. It's found in our trust in people, in their innate capacities and energy. 'I don't know' appears when we are grounded in a higher purpose.

Even if you are not deciding whether to fund a beast-invaded project, you are engaging in leaps of faith involving 'I don't know'. Employing rigorous humility is about embracing and welcoming mystery and continually recreating our work as we learn.

By abandoning chicken-rearing in favour of a paraffin pump, this is exactly what the group in Malawi was attempting to do. I could see that they were in the process of learning from what had happened. Given what they were now proposing, they were clearly engaged in more calculated risk-taking. So why shouldn't I do the same?

Next, when it comes to evidence and measuring results, rigorously humble people exhibit a keen awareness of where they are positioned within the information supply chain. They know how this affects what information is available to them. They consider and make their requests of their partners accordingly.

A few years ago, I was working as the monitoring and evaluation advisor for a regional team at the US-based headquarters of an international organization. There was a big push for project management in the organization and so the regional director decided that it would be best to have monthly reports from the projects' implementers. The funding the regional director provided was to sovereign national-level organizations on another continent.

I didn't disagree with him. Yes, more information about these organizations' activities would be helpful. However the people who reported directly to him, i.e. those more connected to the partner organizations, knew that this was an unreasonable request; a *lot* of bureaucratic hoops would have to be jumped through to make this happen.

As the advisor, I quickly drew up a flowchart that I showed to the regional director. Did he realize that for his request to be fulfilled by volunteers or field officers working on the ground, the report had to pass through eight different levels of approval before it came to him?

No he didn't. He honestly wasn't thinking about that. He told me that he needed to make better financial projections in order to keep funding flowing for the projects. To do this, he told me, he needed more real-time information about what activities were happening and which funds were being spent. Who could argue with this? (Though this monitoring and evaluation advisor was keenly aware we were not even talking about long-term outcomes yet!)

Eventually the team elected to institute monthly check-ins. These phone calls could provide the necessary information to the director. In the process, the team also started to improve relationships due to more frequent interactions with the partner organizations.

There are many layers between funders and where most social-change work is happening – at the community level. No matter the organization or programme in which you're working, rigorous humility requires that we consider what cost and complexity is appropriate for measuring results.

Does a \$5,000 project need the same kind of evaluation as a \$500,000 project? Rigorous humility enables us to also consider what is practical and proportionate given the size and scope of our programmes.

Yes, we have great tools at our disposal to obtain data and information, more than ever before in our history. But that does not mean that we will not need to expect or accept failure or the unexpected. Great tools can be incredibly unhelpful if employed with arrogance or ignorance. Now more than ever, having more information means that we will need to employ rigorous humility to increase our tolerance for the risk of not knowing.

But this is tough medicine to administer to oneself, especially for a person with more power and access to resources. That's why the final characteristic of someone who is rigorously humble is that they consciously surround themselves with people who offer differing perspectives – people with different skills, different backgrounds, and/or more years under their belt.

These critical friends are vital because they help us discover our own blind spots, assumptions, and biases. In other words, if you're a thinker, you need doers around you for a reality check. And for doers, vice versa. Karen Armstrong (2009) describes this as the 'hard work of compassion', or constantly 'dethroning' yourself to challenge your own worldview. This is a vitally-needed skillset that can help cultivate new kinds of institutions. A changing world requires environments with strong incentives for mutual accountability among multiple and diverse stakeholders.

In our lives and in our relationships, it's often the conflicts, the breakdowns, and the mistakes that make us more sure of who we are. These sometimes difficult times are what remind us of our connections to each other, and of what's most important. Those grounded in rigorous humility remind themselves and those around them of this tremendous transformational opportunity.

Conclusion

Here's the bottom line. Anyone can identify what's wrong. But it takes much more skill and strength to wake up every day, and help identify what's right, what's possible, and where incremental changes *can* occur. This is rigorous humility.

Amazing things can happen with more rigorous humility:

- We can invest not just in projects or ideas, but invest in the people who have them – those whose expertise and critical thinking are grounded in their day-to-day, lived experience.
- We can expand the notion of accountability to include not just funders, but the people we serve.
- We can use data for learning, adaptation, and improvement, not compliance, or risk management, or policing.
- We can acknowledge that the information needs of a funder may not be (and usually are not) the same as those working on the ground.

- We can focus on real-time learning and quick adaptation as evidence. Our responsiveness to people's lived realities can be increased.
- We can put just as much or more effort into measuring the strength of our partnerships as we do to following the money trail.
- We can start to see the difference between words on paper and people coming together, willing to be changed by the experience of real dialogue.
- And we can have much more fun!

When planting her garden a few years ago, my grandmother posted this on her Facebook page (yep, I have a pretty hip grandma). She still lives in my hometown of Bruning, Nebraska, a community of less than 300 people in the middle of the US:

> Lillian: *Went to put my tomato cages up that Jr. [my grandpa] had made years ago, they were sitting by our garage. They were gone, guess somebody needed them worse than Me. Enjoy.*

Multiple comments of kind and consoling messages from people in our hometown and beyond appeared:

> *Dislike! I bet they were awesome tomato cages!!!*
> *I put up two rows of combination panels and plant my tomatoes in between ... seems to work well and you can store them away in the winter easier!*
> *Isn't that disappointing? Like you said, somebody needed them worse then you, just hope they REALLY enjoy them.*
> *Bummer, but your reaction to it is beautiful ;)*
> *Sad that someone stole them but what a great attitude you have!!!*
> *Things like that happen all the time down here ... disappointing that it happens in a nice rural community like Bruning!*
> *Sorry to hear that, they were really made well that someone really wanted them ...*

Less than twelve hours later, my grandma posted this update:

> Lillian: *Word got around, my tomato cages walked back home.*

To this day, my grandma doesn't know who took the tomato cages or how they were returned. Does it matter? What matters is that we live in a world where this is possible, especially at the community level.

Why do we need more rigorous humility? Because we cannot let our fears rule our decision-making. Without it, the insistence of certainty and the room for possibility will continue in an inverse relationship. I don't want us involved in the real work of social change to be left asking, 'Where's the faith?'

Rigorous humility leads me to act in ways that acknowledge that people at the grassroots often have the most important expertise in terms of defining and measuring success, often unbeknownst to us who work for organizations attempting to bring about social change.

Undoubtedly, soundly gathered and interpreted data can provide important new information for us all to consider. We should not stop measuring results or searching for evidence, but we do need a dose of rigorous humility. Because often, from where we sit, there remains quite a lot we cannot know. And I, for one, am okay with that.

Summary points

- Fear is a big part of funders' decision making. An overemphasis on data and measuring is an expression of funder's fear of failure and the unknown.
- This unhealthy fixation on metrics has negative consequences on givers and receivers alike.
- Funders' risk-aversion can constrain local leaders' decision-making and responsiveness to communities. Data-gathering or reporting solely for the purpose of accountability to funders fails time and again to result in improvements at the community level.
- Rigorous humility can support funders to unleash more possibilities leading to social change.

About the author

Jennifer Lentfer is director of communications at Thousand Currents (Formerly International Development Exchange – IDEX) <https://www.idex. org> in Berkeley, California, although she is based in Washington DC. She was senior writer of aid effectiveness at Oxfam America from 2012 to 2015, and is the creator of the blog how-matters.org <http://www.how-matters.org>.

Notes

1. Additional details on these methodologies are available within their respective reports and websites: Charity Watch www.charitywatch. org/charitywatch-criteria-methodology; Giving What We Can www. givingwhatwecan.org/get-involved/what-we-can-achieve/; GuideStar www.guidestar.org/rxg/about-us/index.aspx; Philanthropedia http://www. myphilanthropedia.org/how_we_rank; The Life You Can Save http://www. thelifeyoucansave.org/Impact-Calculator; GreatNonProfits www.about. greatnonprofits.org/; Wise Giving Alliance www.give.org/for-donors/ the-care-we-put-into-our-reports/ [All accessed 26 November 2015].
2. Using these methods, organizations like Against Malaria Foundation and Schistosomiasis Control Initiative have been selected as top charities by multiple charity rankers.
3. For a more detailed analysis of the subject, see: Cochrane, L. and Thornton, A. (2015) 'Charity rankings: 'Delivering development or de-humanizing aid?' *Journal of International Development* 28: 57–73.
4. Names and identifying details, and village name, have been changed to protect the privacy of individuals.
5. Mwangi means 'wanderer' in Swahili. Name changed by interviewee to protect identity.
6. Parts of this essay were originally published in *Barefoot Guide 4: Exploring the Real Work of Social Change,* by The Barefoot Collective, 2015, Community Development Resource Association: Cape Town, South Africa. Used with permission.

References

Acton et al. (2009) *Global givers giving locally: A fresh perspective on account-ability,* International Development Capstone Project, George Washington University.

Armstrong, K. (2009) *Charter for compassion* [video], Chautauqua Institution <http://library.fora.tv/2009/08/14/Karen_Armstrong_Charter_for_ Compassion> (posted on 14 August 2009) [Accessed 26 September 2016].

Benkler, Y. (2006) *Wealth of Networks: How Social Production Transforms Markets and Freedom,* Yale, New Haven.

Chambers, R. (2006) *Poverty Unperceived: Traps, Biases and Agenda,* Institute of Development Studies, Brighton.

Cochrane, L. and Thornton, A. (2015) 'Charity rankings: 'Delivering development or de-humanizing aid?' *Journal of International Development* 28: 57–73.

Gamble, C., Ekwaru, J. and ter Kuile, F. (2006) 'Insecticide-treated Nets for Preventing Malaria in Pregnancy', *Cochrane Database of Systematic Reviews* 2006: 2 <http://onlinelibrary.wiley.com/doi/10.1002/14651858.CD003755. pub2/abstract>

Gandhi, M. (1993) *An autobiography: the story of my experiments with truth,* Beacon, Boston, MA.

Gates, B. (2013) *My Annual Letter* [online]. Bill and Melinda Gates Foundation. Available from: <https://www.gatesnotes.com/~/media/Files/Personal/ 2013-Annual-Letter/2013_AL_English.pdf> [Accessed 26 September 2016].

Glassman, A. and Sakuma, Y. (2013) 'How many bed nets equal a saved life? – Why results matter for value for money' in *Center for Global Development Global Health Policy Blog* [blog] <http://www.cgdev.org/blog/how-many-bed-nets-equal-life-saved-%E2%80%93-why-results-matter-value-money> (posted 27 September 2013) [Accessed 14 November 2015].

GlobalGiving (2015) 'About' [website] <www.globalgiving.org/aboutus> [Accessed 14 November 2015].

How Matters (2011) 'If I had only known …' in *How Matters* [blog] <http://www.how-matters.org/2011/03/30/if-i-had-only-known> (posted 30 March 2011) [Accessed on 26 September 2016].

International Monetary Fund (IMF) (2015) *Republic of Congo. Country Report No. 15/264*, International Monetary Fund, Washington.

International Telecommunications Union (2009) *Measuring the Information Society 2009: The ICT Development Index*, International Telecommunications Union, Geneva.

IT News Africa (2009) 'Safaricom's M-Pesa Wins Global Service Award' *IT News Africa*, <http://www.itnewsafrica.com/?p=2263> (posted 19 February 2009) [accessed 29 September 2016].

Krishna, A. (2010) *One Illness Away: Why People Become Poor and How They Escape Poverty*, Oxford University Press, New York, p. 108.

Lengeler, C. (2009) 'Insecticide-treated Nets Can Reduce Deaths in Children by One Fifth and Episodes of Malaria in Half' *Cochrane Database of Systematic Reviews* 2004: 2 <http://onlinelibrary.wiley.com/doi/10.1002/14651858.CD000363.pub2/full>

Lowell, S., Trelstad, B. and Meehan, B. (2005) 'The ratings game: Evaluating the three groups that rate the charities,' *Stanford Social Innovation Review* 39–45.

Mitchell, G. (2014) 'Creating a philanthropic marketplace through accounting, disclosure, and intermediation', *Public Performance & Management Review* 38: 23–47.

Natsios, A. (2010) 'The clash of the counter-bureaucracy and development' in Center for Global Development [essay] <http://www.cgdev.org/publication/clash-counter-bureaucracy-and-development> (posted 1 July 2010) [Accessed 26 September 2016].

Onim J.F. (2002) *Scoping Study for Urban and Peri-Urban Livestock Keepers in Kisumu City, Kenya* [unpublished paper].

Ottenhoff, B. and Ulrich, G. (2012) 'Three steps to more informed giving' in Standford Social Innovation Review [blog] <http://ssir.org/articles/entry/three_steps_to_more_informed_giving> (posted 19 March 2012) [Accessed 26 November 2015].

Ramalingam, B., Miguel, L. and Primrose, J. (2014) *From Best Practice to Best Fit: Understanding and Navigating Wicked Problems in International Development*, Overseas Development Institute, London.

PART V

Smart Risk Number 5: Practicing vulnerability

One of the bravest things we can do as grantmakers is to get out of the driver's seat. Listening to community members, seeking explanations rather than judging, recognizing the privilege we have as outsiders, leads to more lasting change.

Keywords: organizational learning; philanthropy; privilege; accountability; grantmaking

CHAPTER 24
The dissonance

Nora Lester Murad

What if international funders and local, grassroots organizations shared their real perspectives about one another?

***

As a 'local', I've often found it frustrating to communicate with international NGOs and donors.

As an 'international', I've often found it frustrating to communicate with local NGOs.

I don't like the idea that I judge them, but I suppose I do. They say they want to support good local organizations in developing contexts, but their ways of thinking and acting are very problematic.

I don't like the idea that I judge them, but I suppose I do. They say they want our support, and we dedicate our careers to helping them, but they often make it much harder than it has to be.

Sometimes I think we're worse off with their 'help' than we would be without it.

Sometimes I think we'd accomplish more if we just did the work ourselves.

In one, not atypical, case, we heard about an international NGO that gives small, flexible grants to organizations like ours. On their website, they had a long list of grants to organizations in our country. They even had a note – in our language – explaining that they like to make personal connections with their grantees. So we sent them an email. They sent back eight pages of guidelines that were already on their website.

In one, not atypical, case, a local NGO wrote to me: 'We need money'. What does need have to do with anything? I thought. There is far more need than we could ever respond to. They should tell me why I should fund them and not another NGO. I sent them our guidelines (which are on the website, if they had only looked). They didn't even thank me!

We gave the guidelines to a student to translate for us. She did a few pages but when her brother was seriously injured in the war, she started coming

http://dx.doi.org/10.3362/9781780449302.024

to us less and less. We finally managed to translate the guidelines using the internet, and we wrote our responses and translated them on the internet. Some of the questions didn't make sense, though. We skipped the one about inputs, the one about quantitative indicators and the one about social return on investment. We had no idea what they were talking about.

I didn't hear from them for months and then I got a half-proposal. Some of the questions were answered and some weren't, and the English was so poor! Can't they get a proofreader so that I get a decent impression of their capacity? I thought.

Months went by and we didn't hear from the international NGO. They never even acknowledged receiving our proposal! We figured they were like the others – they only give to their friends.

Since I had loads of work, I put their proposal in the order it was received, and when I got to it, there was still enough time for them to get into the next funding round. I sent pages of detailed comments so they could resubmit. Again, no response. Infuriating! They asked me for money and then are non-responsive.

Then, we got an email in which they sent back our proposal. *Did that mean we were under consideration?* We waited. After a long time, we got two emails asking if we planned to submit. They came on the same day right after our weekend, as if we were supposed to answer when the office was closed. We were confused. Hadn't we already submitted? We called the student we knew to come in to explain what the donor wanted. She couldn't come but sent a friend of hers whose English wasn't any better than ours. But we had luck! There was a foreigner sitting in the cafe outside our office. We asked him to read the emails and explain if our proposal was approved or rejected or still being considered. He said the donor had put comments on our proposal, but the comments weren't visible because our software was too old to be compatible with hers. He got the file on his phone. The donor had a comment on every single sentence of our proposal, but not one was about our project – only about the way we explained it. The whole thing was tiring, but we really needed the money. The war had intensified and no one else was giving the kind of services we were giving. Didn't she realize how urgent the situation was? We decided to ask her for a meeting, since we heard from other NGOs that she was coming to our town, though she herself had not told us.

They missed the deadline, and I felt sorry that I had wasted my time. But then I heard from them right before my next trip to the field. They wanted to meet. My schedule was already full with back-to-back meetings, but trying to be a nice person, I added an appointment at 6 p.m.

She gave us a meeting at 6 p.m. We had to go home to cook, supervise our children's homework, make sure our husbands approved, and go back out at night to meet the donor. She held her meetings in the restaurant of a fancy hotel. She bought us tea and cake but we would have rather had the cash for our programs since it was so overpriced. The woman seemed very interested in our work, but even after we explained everything in detail, she still wanted us to fill out all those papers and respond to her comments.

It was a good meeting. They were really nice women and I liked the work they were doing. I wanted to fund them and I had the money, but even weeks later I hadn't managed to get them to send the proposal! I sent an email to ask if they planned to submit. I sent another the next day. No response. I finally just filled in the blanks for them and put my reputation on the line to get them preliminary approval from our management team.

We only have a few people in the office and everyone is dealing with war victims, and we hadn't figured out how to fill out all those papers.

The NGO thanked me, but I really don't think they realized how much effort I put in on their behalf.

But an amazing thing happened! They approved our grant! They just wanted a budget from us.

But in order to get their money, they still needed to prepare the budget. I waited for it and waited for it. The budget guidelines are very clear and easy, but again they missed the next funding deadline.

The foreigner from the cafe agreed to do it for us, but he was called away to another part of the country for his job, and it took a while for him to come back. He finally filled the budget form the way the donor wanted it and we sent it.

I felt like they'd taken advantage of me, and I vowed not to fund them. But when they finally got me their budget, it was fabulous! I pushed through the grant and crossed my fingers that their reporting would be good too. Sadly, it wasn't.

When the money came, we used every penny to help the refugees from the war. Even though it was a very small amount of money, no amount of information was good enough for them.

I spent so much time trying to get better reports from them, I couldn't support as many other local organizations as I wanted to. I even tried to give them extra visibility – giving them the chance to be highlighted in our annual report, on our website, in press releases. But getting information from them was like pulling teeth.

The donor kept sending emails asking for more and more information, statistics, case studies and articles.

Do they really think we just give money without any accountability? Don't they know that I am being held accountable?

Do they really think we just survive to give them reports? Don't they know we are busy trying to meet the increasing needs of our community?

***

What if funder–grantee communications included honest exchanges and principled practices that reflect a commitment to challenge power differentials?

About the author

Nora Lester Murad is a writer and activist in Jerusalem, Palestine. She co-founded Dalia Association <http://www.dalia.ps>, Palestine's community foundation and Aid Watch Palestine <http://www.aidwatch.ps>. She writes about international aid, community philanthropy and life under military occupation at <http://www.noralestermurad.com>.

CHAPTER 25
Uncomfortable conversations

Jennifer Lentfer

Below all of the talk of 'evidence-based approaches' and 'taking interventions to scale' in international aid, philanthropy, social enterprise, and impact investing, there is an undercurrent of disquiet.

It happens when local partners capacity' is maligned. It happens when two people have the same idea, but it is considered legitimate only when the white guy in the room offers it. It happens when people of colour are passed over for leadership positions, jobs, promotions, or pay rises. It happens when different opinions would be helpful, but perspectives are not asked for, or are discounted. It happens when only 1 per cent of humanitarian relief funds make their way to national organizations in Haiti, in West Africa to fight Ebola, and now in Nepal (Carstensen and Els, 2016; Troutman, 2015). It happens when people of colour are assumed to have a lower job status than they do and are treated as such. It happens with every unclosed feedback loop and every feedback loop not yet opened. It happens when the stories and photos we use to describe our work reinforce harmful stereotypes and strip people of their identities.

People's experiences of everyday racism – and the resulting anger, powerlessness, fear, humiliation, and sadness – are not just fleeting instances. They accumulate. And the resulting frustration can result in deep hopelessness in a social-good sector that is supposed to be about equality, fairness, and lifting each other up. The very premise of our industry – that others should live as those in the 'developed world' do – has to be acknowledged and exorcised.

It's time for some uncomfortable conversations.

I hear plenty of conversations about risk, or rather mitigating it in our sector – over and over, in fact. But we need to take the next step and talk about control and power. Who has it? Historically, how did they get it? Systemically, how do they use it? And as a result, who is *not* welcome at the table when decisions are made?

I'm uncomfortable talking about this. Going under the surface is scary. But unless we open up the conversation on racism, sexism, and privilege in the social-good sector, we will continue to perpetuate the same, tired system and make the same mistakes – ones that, right now, we believe can be solved by best practices and improved indicators of success.

http://dx.doi.org/10.3362/9781780449302.025

If our work is not beholden to the love and unity that is possible between people, what *are* we doing? How can our work be re-organized in service of this? Can we stop trying to control projects through logframes, and instead get serious about what it takes to end imperialism and racism and sexism and homophobia and prejudice of all kinds?

When we face uncertainty in the global development sector, we have two choices. We can design (make abstract) and manage (control), or we can inquire (make real) and listen (let go). When our sector focuses our language, our meetings, our reports only the first option, we are too protected by the abstractions of our lexicon. We can too easily claim our commitment to 'results' or 'locally-led development' and too easily skip over the racism at the root of the problems we seek to address, and the prejudices that colour the solutions we profess.

Every time I go to a conference and see a sea of white faces talking about 'their' help to poor, brown people in the global South, I see how much work needs to be done. Our sector does so well at ignoring 'the political', but that has got to change, starting with me.

Do-gooder, over-thinking, and technocratic types (myself included in all three of these categories) fancy ourselves adept at asking the challenging questions of ourselves and of our organizations. But that is no longer enough. We must take concrete actions that dismantle the internal and external power structures that perpetuate inequality and bigotry in non-profits, international aid, philanthropy, social enterprise, and impact investing.

It's time for some uncomfortable conversations. Forgive me for the mistakes I will surely make ...

Summary points

- The social good sector is supposed to be about equality, fairness, and lifting each other up, and it is also about control, power and privilege.
- It is too easy to claim our commitment to results or locally-led development without going deeper.
- We can begin by being honest about the practices that perpetuate inequality and bigotry in non-profits, international aid, philanthropy, social enterprise, and impact investing.

About the author

Jennifer Lentfer is director of communications at Thousand Currents (formerly International Development Exchange – IDEX) <https://www. idex.org> in Berkeley, California, although she is based in Washington DC. She was senior writer of aid effectiveness at Oxfam America from 2012 to 2015, and is the creator of the blog how-matters.org <http://www. how-matters.org>.

CHAPTER 26
Ten rules for helping[1]

The Barefoot Guide Connection

> *People have to be seen as being actively involved, given the opportunity, in shaping their own destiny, and not just as passive recipients of the fruits of cunning development programmes* – Amartya Sen (1999).

People were developing long before international assistance came into their lives and will continue to develop long after it leaves. The will to develop is innate, inborn. It is an inside-out and continuous process. It may not be happening in a healthy or productive way in this or that community, and it may be that its potential is blocked or buried by a series of constraints, but it is the only game in town.

Development is already happening and, as an outsider, I cannot deliver development to anyone – or indeed bring change to anyone – any more than I can eat for them or cough for them! People can only change themselves. Any change that is forced on people is likely to be unsustainable or unhealthy.

In the Letsema Programme we support the rural women's groups to bring their leaders together for five-day workshops. These are not training sessions but development sessions where the women are encouraged to tell their life stories, to listen to each other, to experiment with asking better questions, to inquire into the power relationships they are caught in, and to build trust and solidarity between them. There is very little teaching, just the odd concept or two, and no fixed curriculum.

The workshop moves as the women suggest, increasingly facilitating themselves and setting the agenda. They are continually encouraged to reflect on themselves, to draw strength, forgiveness, and learning from lives that, without exception, are filled with experiences of hardship, trauma, sacrifice, initiative, and triumph. In a few days they start to look at themselves and each other differently, each a bit taller, their eyes filled with hope and courage, and their minds with new ideas.

Do we have the patience and faith to support and let people find and learn from each other in their own way and time?

http://dx.doi.org/10.3362/9781780449302.026

The Taranaki rules

By Warren Feek of The Communication Initiative Network, contributor to the Barefoot Guide

Guidelines for supporting people from the outside who ask, 'Can you please help us to develop a strategy, plan a programme, review some work, write a document, critique a situation, solve a problem ...?' I often get these kinds of 'can you please help/support' requests, whether from a member of a local community group or a leader of a major international organisation.

But being put into the position of outside helper, I can easily do more harm than good. As the centre of gravity of local, national, and international development moves to more local and national decision-making and control, the numbers of such requests are also rapidly growing. There are also more requests for peer support, with a priority on South-South support and cooperation. The world is asking for more collaborative learning and working approaches, and less top-down expertise.

And so, I have developed a set of ten rules that I seek to follow when in a please-help/support situation. I call them the 'Taranaki rules' after my home province in New Zealand. Many of them are grounded in small-community contexts and experience. Of course I break the rules below all the time. And each time I do so I kick myself and try to learn from the experience!

1. **The 'I am a guest' rule**
   The spaces where I am engaged are usually not my community, my country, or my organisation. They are 'owned' by others. I am there as their guest and I need to be a good guest. I am in their space and I will affect that space, and so I should always respect and enhance that space.

2. **The 'I get to leave' rule**
   Though they have very kindly asked me to be involved, or have accepted my involvement, in the end I get to depart that community, country, or organisation – that space. I need to remember that it is not me who will have to pick up the pieces afterwards.

3. **The '90/10 knowledge' rule**
   No matter how much I may think or be told that I know about a situation, issue, dynamic, or problem, I can only know a maximum of 10 per cent, while 'the locals' know about 90 per cent. Often this knowledge is hidden or not valued. This applies to even the most technical of topics. So, I try to create space for the authentic surfacing, valuing, peer sharing, and examination of that local knowledge.

4. **The '10 per cent talk' rule**
   If I am talking more than 10 per cent of the time, I am doing a really poor job (and I can talk!). If I dominate with my 'knowledge', I close the space for engagement, sharing, learning, and creativity, and I begin to undermine rather than help.

5. **The 'four out of five are questions' rule**

Questions open up spaces for engagement. As an outsider, I may be able to ask some different questions that open up a process – questions that create space for new or different understandings or relationships. So I try to ensure that my questions outnumber any specific ideas or statements I may share by a ratio of 4 to 1.

6. **The 'marginal voices' rule**

As an outsider in a process, I am less hidebound by pre-existing dynamics such as who gets to speak most, or whose opinion carries the most weight. Trying to change the dynamics in the space means respectfully encouraging the quieter, 'less important' voices to surface and be acknowledged.

7. **The 'would you mind sharing your story with us' rule**

My culture places high value on getting down to business as quickly as possible, but this is not always a good way for an outsider to work. So I try to create time and space for people to share their stories. It is amazing what even close colleagues or neighbours do not know about each other. The inclusion of personal elements creates a closer and more meaningful space for understanding and working with each other.

8. **The 'five-year' rule**

People struggle to look past the day-to-day problems, opportunities and worries, and to have a long-term view. When it feels appropriate, I ask everyone to outline where they want to be in five years time in relation to the priority issues on the table. This is an attempt to raise the group's gaze and direct their actions to longer-term solutions, rather than just fighting fires.

9. **The 'when to share my ideas and proposals' rule**

I get invited to give support because I am regarded as having some technical knowledge and expertise that can be helpful. Everything in rules 1 to 8 above works against that happening! So I have a dilemma. My rules for when to share my ideas and proposals revolve around being asked at least three times by three different people; being substantively into the process that is underway; having sufficient time left for my ideas or proposals to be critically examined; and, being able to explain them using the analysis emerging from the process to date. Timing is critical.

10. **The 'what agenda or plan' rule**

If you are 25 per cent of the way into a support/help process and the opening agenda or plan is still being followed – well, that is not good!

About the author

The Barefoot Guide Connection <http://www.barefootguide.org> is a global and local community of social change leaders and practitioners.

CHAPTER 27
Whose capacity needs to be built?

Jennifer Lentfer

Often people are attracted to a mystified or romanticized idea of 'making a difference'. But inequality, injustice, and poverty have deep roots. Thus solutions don't magically appear with the introduction of a new person, idea, or resources – and they certainly don't happen overnight.

But if people can be open to reflection and learning along the way, then something can happen – that aha! moment where you see social-change work is complex, and it can never be simple again.

Today there are more and more ways that allow people to get money directly to people and projects on the ground. But moving money is not quite as sexy as feeding children on mission trips, is it? That's the dilemma.

'Capacity building' has been in every job description or programmatic strategy of every international aid and philanthropic organization with which I've worked over the past 15 years. In some form or another, I've led, funded, or facilitated workshops, exchange visits, and training intended to enhance the knowledge and skills of people who live in poor countries.

Given that I was born in a so-called modern society, my capacity has rarely been at question as an expat aid worker, as a grant maker, as a manager, and a communicator. It's assumed I have inherent skills, knowledge, abilities, and resources since I'm not from a 'traditional' society.

But when I think back to that 19-year-old university student who, on her first trip out of the United States, went to volunteer at an orphanage ... wow, talk about someone who needed her capacity built!

When I think back to that budding aid worker, newly arrived from her master's programme, ready to use all that development 'expertise', only to find that many of her Zimbabwean colleagues had a master's in development too, and way more experience ... wow, did her capacity need to be built!

All along my career, there have been big, bold examples of ineptitude and small moments of self-doubt. And they didn't subside as I gained more experience. Rather they multiplied in many ways. Doing things 'the way they'd always been done' in international grant making actually wasn't working for anyone.

And, as I supported more and more effective indigenous-led organizations, I saw the vision, structure, and impact they were having – with or without funding or support from outsiders like me. Rather than focusing on what

http://dx.doi.org/10.3362/9781780449302.027

wasn't there, I came to appreciate the inherent strengths of local leaders: their deep contextual knowledge, embeddedness within the community, ingenuity in stretching resources, and the ability to operate in a manner responsive to local needs.

And I realized, over and over again, that if I was going to be a vital part of supporting bottom-up development, global social justice, and grassroots-driven social change, I needed to build my capacity to support these effective, inspiring, and visionary leaders. I needed more than cultural competence – I needed cultural humility. I needed to know how to build authentic and more equal partnerships with community-based organizations and grassroots movements. I needed to know how to form and foster networks of learning, mutual support, and solidarity.

Perhaps the ability and penchant to understand and work with organizations of any size and type can and should become a core skill of anyone working on behalf of social change. We need funders, aid practitioners, social entrepreneurs, and do-gooders thinking carefully and differently about what it is to do justice to people's vast and vital efforts around the world.

What do people need to develop? Technical assistance, oversight, and inspection? Or resources, solidarity, and encouragement?

Thank goodness for many, many aha! moments that have passed, and for the many inevitably to come!

Summary points

- The assumption of a lack of capacity is not ahistorical, nor apolitical.
- Outsiders and funders need their capacity built too.
- Working with organizations of any type or size should become part of the do-gooders toolbox.

About the author

Jennifer Lentfer is director of communications at Thousand Currents (Formerly International Development Exchange – IDEX) <https://www.idex.org> in Berkeley, California, although she is based in Washington DC. She was senior writer of aid effectiveness at Oxfam America from 2012 to 2015, and is the creator of the blog how-matters.org <http://www.how-matters.org>.

CHAPTER 28

Questions to focus organizational learning for social change

The Barefoot Guide Connection

Many organisations aspire to be learning organisations but there is very little practical guidance available, except from the business world. That guidance is difficult to interpret and apply to the more complex terrain of social change, and often guided by different priorities. The purpose of becoming a learning organisation is to become more effective in our work, to improve our practice in the field. Some of us might say, 'Oh we know what our practice is already; it's in our strategic plans, so let's move onto the next question ...' But wait a bit. It makes good sense to begin by revisiting our practice, to remind ourselves, collectively, what our real work is. As a proposed way forward, I have outlined below several of the most important areas on which you could focus organisational learning.

Developing a purpose and theories of change

What really matters to us? Where we can make our most useful contribution to the world?

Understanding what social change is

Deepening the theories of change that connect the work we do with the contribution we want to make.

Developing practical approaches, strategies, and methods for specific interventions, programmes, or projects

What is the real need, and our real work, in this situation? What have we learned from experience here so far, and what does it mean for our next action? How can we improve our approach to this situation? What can we learn from others?

Giving and receiving feedback

How can we help people to see and understand their contribution and to get helpful and specific feedback through which they can learn, both individually and collectively? How can feedback be received as a gift (even if challenging) and not a criticism?

http://dx.doi.org/10.3362/9781780449302.028

Building specific skills

What skills need to be strengthened? What skills need to be acquired?

Building good support systems and procedures

How can we design our support systems and procedures to serve the needs and to suit the realities of our practice?

Innovating and designing

How can we encourage innovation, creativity, and risk-taking? How can we use our collaborative potential to spark new ideas, designs, and initiatives?

Overcoming conflicts and resentments

How can we surface and deal with conflict and resentments?

Building authentic community

How can we regularly renew relationships and enthusiasm for working together? How can we pay attention to the emotional health of the organization and its people?

Developing healthy living and working paths

How can we help people, as individuals, to vision and plan their working lives and to grow themselves more fully as human beings? How can we help them to find healthy balances between work and personal lives?

About the author

The Barefoot Guide Connection <http://www.barefootguide.org> is a global and local community of social change leaders and practitioners.

CHAPTER 29
What happens when we listen?

Rajasvini Bhansali

It had been six months since I had started my new role as a management advisor for a network of youth polytechnics[2] in rural Kenya. The Wakamba village elders in Maseki village where I lived had named me Mutanu meaning 'one who smiles a lot'. My career, coursework, and volunteer training in management consulting, policy analysis, community organizing, and organizational development, had prepared me well for the task.

Or so I thought.

Within the first few weeks, it was apparent that one of the youth polytechnics had some serious management challenges. While all the polytechnics in the district were resource-strapped, with underpaid teachers and impoverished students, at least the others had sound leadership and community buy-in. I saw it in parents' willingness to sell a parcel of land to pay for their children's education.

But this one (we'll call it 'KYP') never seemed to retain any equipment or students or teachers. Each month, we heard of a new burglary and little by little, all the 'assets' of the institution were disappearing.

In the meantime, the principal of the polytechnic appeared to be getting richer. He had built a home for himself, lavish by local standards, and was able to send his children away for higher education, while the polytechnic he ran struggled to survive. It did not take long for me to come to the conclusion that he was embezzling funds, and possibly even organizing these burglaries. The murmurs about his character at the town market only seemed to confirm my suspicions.

So I shared my concerns with the coordinating committee of the district's network of polytechnics. Mr M, a local teacher and community leader, was my direct supervisor in my 'capacity building' role. Time after time, I would bring up my animated allegations about how criminal and unethical the KYP principal's behaviour was. And each time, Mr M would patiently nod, listen to all my rants and then say, 'We shall address.'

Another week or two would go by, nothing would change, and I would get more and more frustrated. To me, there was no time to waste in seeing the principal of KYP fired and a new principal found. I was convinced that I couldn't be effective in working with the network of polytechnics unless the right people were in place. Despite all I knew about cultural competence,

http://dx.doi.org/10.3362/9781780449302.029

I found myself falling prey to that often-circulated notion that people in the global South, particularly in Africa, are conflict-averse and slow or reluctant to handle corruption issues.

After a few months of my fruitless ranting and what I deemed inaction, Mr M finally called a meeting of community leaders at the struggling KYP. The principal under investigation was also present. After the first hour of pleasantries, tea, small talk, and general discussion about the community, I was becoming impatient.

In my head, I continued to worry about their lack of confrontation with this man, who so clearly deserved to be brought to justice. But at least I had learned something in my first six months in Kenya – sometimes my most important role was observer.

As the conversation continued well into the second hour, I noticed that Mr M was skillfully and patiently changing the course of the conversation. He spoke slowly and confidently, sharing that the community had a problem and the problem was the inability of one of our institutions to do justice to our children's education. He spoke without any air of malice or judgment of the principal.

This collective ownership of what appeared to one man's and one polytechnic's problem helped me pause my internal narrative. What transpired in the room after this shift in the conversation transformed how I have thought about and worked on organizational and leadership development ever since.

The elders sat in silence and invited the principal to reflect on his part in the community's troubles. Mr M posed gentle, yet sobering questions in a spirit of reflection, subtlety and powerfully appealing to his sense of shared responsibility to address the polytechnic's ongoing struggles. Initially, the principal got defensive, even angry, but Mr M continued with his questions. Each one carried the principal to a new level of awareness. Each word offered by the elders demonstrated to the principal the implications of his action for the whole community.

This process of reflection, silence, then call to the collective good continued for another few hours. The principal's anger turned into reflection and then tears. As he broke down, he not only owned up to embezzlement, but also to having let down his own family, his community, his people, and the generations to come. As the fifth hour of our meeting drew to a close, the principal made a pledge to return the funds, apologize in public, and to move on and make space for a new leader.

After the meeting, I was in awe of what Mr M and the committee members had been able to do. Had the principal been approached with derision and singled out and punished as I would have initially liked to see, he perhaps would have just gone on to create the same mess elsewhere. But Mr M and the elders were not guided by their anger. Had they been, they would have denied the principal an opportunity for healing and for redemption.

Box 29.1 Did I …?

By Jennifer Lentfer

No matter how you relate to your role in making the world a more equitable and peaceful place for its people to share in its prosperity, you have to do the internal work to know yourself first. Self-reflection is important for creating and maintaining sound relationships. Select a period of time, and ask yourself the following:

- Did I embrace change, or resist it? Did I welcome challenges and seize opportunities, or shrink from them? When did I push myself outside of my comfort zone? What have I done recently for the first time?
- To what, or whom, did I give power? What kinds of power (personal, positional and institutional) did I use to change the status quo?
- What kind of leader am I? Did I let generosity lead me, or fear? Did I remember how small (and powerful) I am?
- Did I let the 'musts, shoulds, and have-tos' rule me? When did I question 'the rules', especially when they hurt people?
- How am I walking in solidarity? Am I offering the kinds of support to the local and global movements that will transform our society?
- How did I challenge my own biases, -isms, and pre-conceived notions? How did I wear my privilege?
- Did I find out, or did I suppose? Did I listen, or speak more? Was I able to observe without evaluating?
- When did I embrace risk, or did I value too much the logic, the odds, the compliments?
- Did I make up my own mind, or care too much about what others think?
- Did I reject perfect? (What a fallacy!)
- Where did I dally too long? Did I exhaust all possibilities?
- What fascinated me? Where and when did I encounter wonder? Where did I find the ridiculous, the silly?
- What did I celebrate?
- What did I have the courage to ask for? When did I ask for help? When did I ask for feedback? When could I have asked sooner? Did I receive with grace?
- Was I my own hero, or was I too busy saving others?
- Did I allow myself to rest and find peace, or did I focus too much on 'productivity'? Did I do enough to nourish my body, my heart, my creativity, my soul?
- Did I give myself permission to say 'no' often enough?
- How did I conduct myself between the amazing and the awful, the peaceful and the wild? How did I walk through the ordinary, the routine, the mundane?
- How often did I notice the beautiful souls around me? Who did I look at, but not see?
- Did I lift up what connects us, rather than what divides us? Did I give my 'enemies' chances to become my allies and collaborators?
- Was I an enthusiast, or a naysayer?
- Did I walk in the world with my heart, or use my head as a battering ram?
- Did I make enough mistakes? Did I let myself and others learn from them? Did I own up to what I did/do not know? Did I allow myself to be taught by everyone and everything around me?
- Could I have tread more softly on this precious earth?
- Was I light in a dark world?

Instead, they choose to preserve the sense of collective responsibility that bound them as a network and as a committee, while offering the principal an opportunity to preserve his personal dignity. I learned that criminalizing is short term and less effective than the process of lasting community accountability.

I am fortunate that now in my role as executive director of Thousand Currents (formerly IDEX), I am engaged with an approach to international social-change philanthropy and impact investing that builds the power of grassroots groups and their local leaders. Looking back to my time in Kenya, I now know I was learning what it means to be a self-aware practitioner: to listen deeply, to not intervene prematurely, to have deep respect for the process of change and empowerment, to resist the temptation to be an expert, and instead accompany the process of development.

Often, when I look in the mirror and get real with myself about how I'm behaving as a leader, I remember Mr M's kind and patient face – ready to listen first, build unity, and then act with compassion.

And then I remember, I still have a long way to go.

Summary points

- Our internal narratives affect our work greatly. Our biases show up.
- Being a self-aware practitioner means: listening deeply, not intervening prematurely, having deep respect for the process of change and empowerment, resisting the temptation to be an expert, and instead accompanying the process of development.
- When we are led by people who know the context better than ourselves, we don't disrupt collective processes for decision-making and accountability. Instead, we can uphold and witness healing.

About the author

Rajasvini Bhansali is executive director of Thousand Currents <https://www.idex.org> (formerly called IDEX – International Development Exchange) in Berkeley, California. USA.

CHAPTER 30

The five essential qualities of grassroots grantmakers

Jennifer Astone

The first grant I ever received was a colossal failure.

It was 1986 and I was a Peace Corps volunteer. On behalf of a women's group in rural Senegal, I applied for a Trickle Up grant to establish a half-hectare mango orchard. The terms of the grant were clear: if the application were approved, the group would receive a US$50 cheque. A second US$50 cheque would be sent upon receipt of a progress report after six months.

I had discussed the orchard with the women for months. They would plant and water specially-grafted mango seedlings that fruited later in the season than the local variety. They agreed to protect the trees from free-ranging cattle and goats with a fence. Delighted with the project and its potential, I was sure the orchard would even out their fruit production and provide them with both food and a new source of income.

Several months later, when the cheque arrived, the women gathered huge wooden stakes and dug postholes. Their husbands and sons helped them plant the tender seedlings in the half-fenced plot. But just at the moment when I thought the orchard might be enclosed, the first rains arrived. Everyone turned their attention to preparing their corn, rice, and millet fields, instead of completing the mango orchard fence. Free-ranging cows and goats ravaged the unprotected seedlings. I was devastated. Through the Peace Corps, I hoped to help poor communities, but I had gotten it all wrong. My agenda and the schedule I pushed for did not mesh with local priorities.

Over the next year and a half, I pondered the lessons of that failed US$50 grant and incorporated them into the next project. In my second year, I had become more fluent in the vernacular language and I spent time learning more about local agricultural practices, visiting nearby villages and meeting the local government representatives focused on health, agriculture and women's issues.

As I spent more time alongside the women in Senegal's rice paddies and the men in the peanut fields, I saw first-hand the toll taken by malaria. Mothers and fathers lost valuable farming days lying in bed sick or walking miles to the clinic, carrying a feverish infant. As a Peace Corps volunteer, I had access to a prophylactic medicine to prevent malaria that cost pennies. The government

http://dx.doi.org/10.3362/9781780449302.030

of Senegal also made this medicine available in health clinics. But people did not have easy access to malaria prevention and treatment because they did not have a trusting relationship with the health clinic personnel.

A nurse at the nearby clinic and I established a distribution programme to enable pregnant women and the elderly, those at highest risk from malaria, from seventeen villages to purchase the medicine from the clinic. Individuals within communities paid for the medicine themselves. Local leaders, literate in Arabic, recorded the participants and monitored the medication. No outside funds were required. The villagers were proud to run their own programme; they gained a sense of control over their health outcomes and developed close relationships with regional health clinic staff.

I learned that the government of Senegal and UNICEF had started a national childhood vaccination programme that year. It was leaving mothers in my area confused by transient post-vaccination fevers, and sceptical about the need for age-dependent booster shots. This small health programme led me to understand that better communication with the communities and local health officials could improve mothers' participation in this important programme.

So the nurse and I then planned a three-day health workshop. We solicited a small grant of US$300 to cover participation by representatives from twelve villages. The workshop explained the basics of the prevention and treatment of malaria and diarrhoea, as well as the value of vaccinations. I had already learned how it was the tradition that people be segregated in public interaction by gender; thus, we required each village to send one woman and one man to the workshop to ensure that the health information would reach all of the adults in each participating village. While the necessity of segregating male and female posed accommodation challenges, both the men and women eagerly engaged in the learning sessions. People took time from their work, arranged for child care, and voiced their concerns about what was most needed. The three-day workshop succeeded because we started with local needs, involved local health officials, accommodated community cultural practices, and valued community priorities in establishing the programme's goals.

In the village where I lived, many of the granaries, grain mills, and health promotion projects failed, just as the mango orchard had failed, because government ministries, international agencies and non-governmental actors failed to engage deeply with the community. Experts developed these interventions as 'replicable models' to reach the intended wider scale and to move the large sums of money required by large donors. The whole process appeared backwards.

Imagine for a moment that you are a programme officer at a large foundation and had a multi-million dollar budget to allocate. Wouldn't it be easier to make one big million-dollar grant for 100 granaries at US$10,000 each instead of creating a small grant mechanism where communities designed their own approach for setting aside grain from their harvest? Perhaps you are also under pressure to reduce the amount of overhead associated with your food-security programme. The ideology of cost-effectiveness means that rarely are you under pressure to make decisions based on which strategy would have more potential to still be working in five or ten years.

Why not rethink the model of pushing money and projects onto communities, and instead let local priorities determine the needs and drive the design and pace of the work?

When the grant seeker becomes the grant giver

It was 2004. I was at my desk reviewing a final report and renewal grant application from a Rwandan street children's programme. After my stint in the Peace Corps, I joined the African Development Foundation as a grants analyst in 1989. I then held a string of progressively more senior jobs that ultimately led to my role as the executive director of the Firelight Foundation, which funded child-focused, community-based organizations in sub-Saharan Africa.

It was up to me to evaluate the street children's programme. Was it effective? Did it have a future? The numbers didn't add up. I couldn't figure out how the new budget correlated with the proposed activities or the number of enrolled kids. From the written word, I couldn't predict whether our grant, should we give it, would support a viable programme or a sinking ship.

I had emailed the director several weeks earlier to seek clarification, and I hadn't received a response. With the deadline for grant recommendations looming, I went into the office at 6a.m. to once again try to reach the director by phone (we had a nine-hour time difference). On the fourth attempt, I finally got through. The connection hissed noisily. After a quick hello, I asked him directly about the budget. The director hesitated.

'We lost our major donor last year.'

My heart sank.

'We managed. Most of the staff remained. They took salary cuts in order to stay with the kids.'

My mind vacillated between admiration for the staff's resolve and worry about the drop in funding.

'We have another grant under review with a new donor not described in our application to you.'

The line cut out. When I called back, the line was busy.

By the time the call went through again, I had rethought my approach. This wasn't all about the numbers. Something else was going on; there was a story behind the work. I asked the director how he had gotten involved.

'Jen, I saw these kids of eight and nine in the streets after the 1994 genocide. I was working for a non-governmental organization at the time, yet no one was helping them. I offered the boys some food and clothes and they began to trust me. It began like that almost seven years ago.'

He told me how he had persuaded the city government to donate land for a residential centre. He had raised funds and recruited staff, but last year the international donor had changed priorities and had withdrawn the funding. That started to explain why the numbers looked so strange.

That's when I knew I had to recommend this programme for continued funding. I was clearly talking to a change-maker, someone who had the persistence to create and sustain a programme for these kids – even when the funds were not available.

A small grant to their organization was exactly the kind of risk I wanted Firelight to make, but I would never have understood that had I relied solely on the written application. What had appeared illogical and unsustainable on paper from an office thousands of miles away was the work of a man with a tenacious streak and a team of committed volunteers and child advocates. Community activists are like that. Grassroots grant programmes are made for leaders like him and the communities they represent.

What people need to run effective grassroots grant programmes

Grassroots grant programmes give donors and foundations a pathway to expand the participation of marginalized communities and activists in building sustainable change, tapping into a rich resource of unrecognized strengths, ideas, and creativity.

But for many foundations, setting up a grassroots grants programme is a quixotic task. In a world of big-dollar philanthropy and impact investing, global small grant programmes attract little attention. And yet it is grants at the community level that can result in empowered leaders and groups, and processes of accountable, participatory, and transformational social change. What to many appears quixotic and unsustainable in practice is the work of grassroots grant makers who, beneath the surface, exhibit an unwavering commitment to relationship and solidarity building.

To be successful, grassroots grant programmes require a well-defined focus, straightforward guidelines, clear accountability systems, and strong feedback processes founded on benefiting people as well as promoting ethical principles. Amidst the daily grind of developing selection criteria, reporting templates and long email chains, we need community organizing experience and a temperament to successfully guide the process *and* create effective relationships with communities, activists, and social entrepreneurs.

Ultimately, we must implement a philanthropic ethic and a practice that embraces local ideas and initiatives. This is uniquely challenging in cultures and nations that are bombarded with outside assistance from outsiders who rarely value their input. That is why a grassroots grants programme is only as good as the people that run it.

I have thought a lot about the expertise, motivation, and self-awareness required of those of us involved in grassroots grant programmes. I've often wondered: Why do our interactions with communities and activists matter so greatly? What characteristics and practices make for successful grassroots grant makers? What best practices should we all embrace?

I have learned a lot in the twenty years I've been involved in grants programmes as grant seeker, and in philanthropy as staff and manager. The reasons why certain actions worked in both settings remained strikingly similar.

Five essential qualities

In a job description in the global development sector, you would expect to find a listing for the following skillsets: field experience, language competence, writing skills, the ability to work well with others, etc. But beyond this, to make grant programmes effective, I value and seek to cultivate five additional qualities in myself and in my staff: curiosity, listening skills, self-awareness, openness/respect, and patience. These are the basis of effective relationships.

Curiosity

Most international aid and philanthropy jobs require a depth of issue-specific knowledge or linguistic competency in a specific geographic area of interest. Anyone working in international aid, however, will admit that despite their experience, communities and issues are essentially heterogeneous. Thus, expertise does not always translate into solutions. Staff members must use their own curiosity to uncover the local history, culture, beliefs, and existing efforts and relationships.

When the orchard failed in Senegal, I had lived in the village as a young, eager Peace Corps volunteer for eight months. I was anxious to start a project, any project. I assumed in suggesting the orchard project that the women would share any challenges we might encounter. I learned later that the most outspoken member of the woman's group had left the village due to a divorce shortly before my arrival, contributing to the women's silence on the timing of the orchard. I did not understand how labour demands peak at certain periods of the year for a community dependent upon rain-fed agriculture. Had I been more curious about the demands on the women's time, I might have discovered that the orchard planting was poorly timed. When the women abandoned the orchard fence, they did not judge it worthless, but instead placed a higher priority on their main occupation as farmers whose rain-fed crops depended upon their timely action.

At the Firelight Foundation, while I had experience making grants in Rwanda, I was unfamiliar with programmes for street children, and had no context within which to place such a programme. I realized I needed to be more curious about the rationale behind the street kids' programme. Because the logic of the programme and budget was not straightforward, I needed to inquire about the founding story and the current situation in order to make a well-reasoned recommendation. Curiosity taught me that written proposals are a mere shadow of the reality they try to portray. Overcoming those limitations meant teasing out the details of the community, organization, and its leadership through phone and email dialogue, local advisor input, programme analysis, and site visits.

Ultimately, we cannot know everything about the community and programmes we fund. Trust is required. We must balance what they can know with what is knowable, and take reasonable risks based on our assessment of the context, community, local leadership, and proposed programmes.

Listening skills

Aid workers, social entrepreneurs, volunteers, funders, outsiders intending to do good, too often arrive in developing countries with a worldview that they have the answers. There are long colonial histories that have built up the supremacy of rich nations' technology, infrastructure, logic, and ideas embedded within a racist paradigm of the superiority of the West and whiteness. Unfortunately, these legacies manifest themselves in people's inability to listen deeply to local perspectives and to follow local priorities. Supporting locally transformative development in which communities harness their resources in sustainable ways means cultivating listening skills and learning to empathize with people.

In Senegal, I observed and listened as villagers spoke about their struggles to access the health care they so desperately needed. I remember one woman's confusion and anger after walking one hour to a vaccination clinic and waiting for three hours, only to have her baby turned away while her neighbour's baby was vaccinated. I could only imagine how frustrating that would be for me. Public health is not all about stocking medicines and building clinics – it requires community involvement, education, and demand.

Listening takes up valuable time. Had I not made the time to listen to the director of the street children's programme, his application wouldn't have proceeded and they would have lost even more funding. If I'd been in too much of a hurry, I would have rejected the application outright. Since one of Firelight's trusted advisors had highly recommended the group, I felt I had to dig deeper to uncover the whole story. I slowed down enough to listen, and what I learned from the director directly increased my confidence in his leadership and in the programme. Practicing active listening, asking questions, and, more importantly, allowing plenty of time for discussion, demonstrates respect.

Listening means also being willing to experience the reality of others. For example, when I visited Rwanda, I did not choose to rent a vehicle to visit Firelight's grantees. Instead, I depended upon partner organizations to arrange transportation. That means that I dealt with late start times. I climbed into old vehicles. I spent time with drivers searching for fuel. Those experiences offered invaluable 'unscheduled' time for connecting and listening to everyday people. It forced me to manage my expectations and, by experiencing local logistical challenges, I had a deeper understanding of the trials of programme implementation.

Self-awareness

Recognizing how my identity as a privileged white, female US citizen fits into the context of a global history of racism and economic exploitation has not been an easy part of my journey, but I see it as critical to any grant maker's success. There are dynamics at play in my funding relationships and so I've had to work on ways to express my respect, understanding, and solidarity with community members.

In the Peace Corps, I learned that I wielded tremendous power. As a young person I didn't expect this. Imagine, I was the only English- and French-literate adult in the village. I could translate an idea onto the page and send it half way around the world to staff at the New York-based Trickle Up, which accepted written applications in English only, not Pular, the language spoken locally, or French. I wrote down my uninformed vision of how the orchard would work, unfettered by local truths. What a position of power – I was the only link between the community and the source of funds!

To get beyond superficialities in my philanthropic career, I ask people for their personal stories and share mine. Discussion always ensues. Sharing my story and what connects me to the work is critical for helping communities and individuals understand my motivation, and vice versa. Sharing my story also demonstrates that I am human and make mistakes. This requires humility and openness. In my case, Trickle Up had lost US$50 on a Peace Corps volunteer's misunderstanding of the labour calendar and over-eager desire to make a difference. My enthusiastic error of judgment taught me a lot.

Self-awareness creates the space for learning from mistakes. People organizing their communities need opportunities to experiment with new ideas, try out activities and ways of working together. Likewise, we need the ability to make adjustments based on incorporating feedback from the local experts.

Openness and respect

When hiking through a lowland tropical forest, an indigenous woman who was serving as my guide explained to me how the police took away her beloved pet monkey. Discriminatory national laws set up to 'protect' wildlife did not respect local practices.

Aren't monkeys supposed to be wild? I thought. I learned that her tribe hunts monkeys for food and views them as part of their daily world. In fact, her communities' interdependence on their biodiverse land base requires both deep knowledge and ongoing resource management to survive. My guide was in direct contact with them on a regular basis. I had only encountered monkeys in zoos.

Later, when the guide told me of her sister's year-long vision quest in the forest, I knew that her spiritual experience outstripped the limits of my worldview, education, and training. My most recent work with indigenous people has shown me ways of honouring the earth and feeling connected to it that are far beyond what my intellectual ability or Western linear thinking can comprehend.

This is not a comfortable place for a grant maker who wants to utilize a clear rationale to make decisions. But I've learned that, when working cross-culturally, if you're never uncomfortable, you are not challenging yourself. There are many ways of 'knowing' and 'learning' in the world.

I have learned from indigenous people to allow for more silence in deliberation, for example, contrary to my habit and cultural conditioning of talking out or brainstorming a solution. Respecting the silence allowed me to connect to another way of being, and to my heart. By sharing a meal, listening to a story, joining in a song, or attending a service at a place of faith, we can show respect for people's struggles, their courage, and leadership. We can also reconnect with our passion for our work and our souls. The willingness to be vulnerable enables us to share our humanity and our solidarity more readily.

Patience

Finally, we need patience. We need patience to endure with good humour a daily routine of small inconveniences. The patience enables us to realize that the kind of change communities and activists desire takes years to achieve. The commitment to stay with a grassroots grants programme over the years ultimately determines the programme's success. Building on relationships over time enables staff to have more open and honest communication with grantees and to identify opportunities that are not readily apparent to outside observers.

How long is too long to support a programme that was going to spend years helping to assist children who had found their way onto the streets? We shortchange ourselves by thinking only in terms of annual reports and three-year project cycles. We must consider how long it takes to see transformative change in the real world.

Patience is paramount.

Conclusion

Cultivating these five qualities equips us to be more effective in our relationships. And this is vital as we face the realities of grassroots grants work, which includes piles of unsolicited applications to review with care; dozens of intermittent email threads to follow up on with advisors and applicants; as well as the expectation to travel to dispersed communities in multiple countries on a limited budget, while experiencing frustrating conditions with grace and insight.

While a focused mission, clear grant criteria, and due-diligence procedures are necessary elements in developing a grassroots grant programme, they cannot dictate how grant makers interact and collaborate with the individuals and communities applying for the grants. These interactions are often, in and of themselves, more important than the structure of any programme. By bringing curiosity, listening skills, self-awareness, openness and respect, and patience to our work, we can bridge the gaps in written applications that do not adequately reflect the complex histories and contexts of the communities and activists we want to support.

Successful grassroots grant programmes depend on people who do not start from a place of thinking that outside experts have the best answers for every community, nor from equating their contribution with the amount of money they manage or give away. Instead grassroots grant makers start where people are, and support the local processes that build upon their unique strengths, resources and ideas. Courage and humility are required to accept that the best solutions often come from communities themselves and not from outsiders.

Relationships, as much as a funder's dollars, is what unleashes those solutions.

Summary points

- The ideology of cost-effectiveness means that rarely are you under pressure to make decisions based on which strategy would have more potential to still be working in five or ten years.
- What can appear illogical and unsustainable on paper from an office thousands of miles away may not fully represent the work of people with a tenacious streak and a team of committed volunteers. Taking time to listen and build relationships cuts through this distrust.
- Five qualities of grant makers can help make programmes more effective: curiosity; listening skills; self-awareness; openness/respect; and patience.

About the author

Jennifer Astone is executive director of Swift Foundation <https://swiftfoundation.org> in California, USA. She was executive director at Firelight Foundation from 2001 to 2008.

Notes

1. This essay was originally published as 'Working with questions? What is our primary role as development practitioners' in *Barefoot Guide 4: Exploring the Real Work of Social Change,* by The Barefoot Connection, 2015, Community Development Resource Association: Cape Town, South Africa, pp. 84–86. Used with permission.
2. Youth polytechnics are vocational training schools created to serve the rural poor so that young people who cannot make it to secondary schools can learn practical skills for employment.

References

Carstensen, N. and Els, C. (2016) 'Where is all the money going? The humanitarian economy', IRIN [website] <http://newirin.irinnews.org/the-humanitarian-economy> [accessed 29 September 2016].

Sen, A. (1999) *Development as Freedom,* Knopf, New York.

Troutman, E. (2015) 'Nepal earthquake $422 million humanitarian response: Less than 1% will go directly to local organizations' in *AirWorks* [blog] <http://aid.works/2015/06/nepal-local-orgs-left-out> (posted 19 June 2015) [accessed 29 September 2016].

Conclusion

Jennifer Lentfer and Tanya Cothran

The challenge now for grantmakers, giving circles, social entrepreneurs, NGO staff, impact investors, grassroots leaders, donors, and philanthropists is to put power back in the hands of marginalized people and communities. When matched with the vision, resolve, and ingenuity of those coming together all over the world, this model is a proven formula for lasting change.

Keywords: Philanthropy; grassroots organizations; aid effectiveness; managing risk; grassroots change

Look up. Look around. The web of community-based organizations, grassroots movements, and local solutions around the world is plentiful. Small, yet formidable, pockets of people-power coming together – these are the building blocks of change.

Taking smart risks means supporting grounded solutions, honouring grassroots leadership, and relying on local knowledge and wisdom. Smart risks means executing our work collaboratively with thoughtfulness, kindness, and creativity.

As the authors have learned from grassroots leaders that it is the quality of the work and not just the quantity of the grant that matters, we are challenging the very notion of 'small'. Small is, in fact, big – big on impact, big on innovation, and big on sustainability. It is for this reason that direct, flexible, and responsive investments in visionary, effective leaders do not pose a high risk to funders.

How can funders take more smart risks?

Look and aim for community accountability

Effective grassroots organizations include community members in planning and in day-to-day decision-making about their activities. In other words, the leaders get their marching orders from the people they serve – not the other way around.

Skilled grassroots grant makers look for groups that demonstrate solid evidence of strong community ownership within their organizations. When this is present, theft and corruption become rarer because there are more eyes on the money. These are eyes of people who feel accountable to the group and who would consider themselves responsible if the work was unsuccessful.

What if ...?

What if ... when money was being donated, Dianne thought, 'How can I get some of this directly into the hands of grassroots organizations already working on the ground?'

What if ... after she gave, Dianne could develop lasting relationships with vetted and effective local leaders in the global South?

What if ... when a problem or crisis presented itself, Jamie's next thought was, 'Let's see what local leaders have to say?'

What if ... Jamie could devote 10 per cent or 30 per cent or 50 per cent of their budget to grassroots-conceived and -led organizations?

What if ... Jamie re-oriented capacity building approaches for community groups to be rooted in what they most require from us – allies, nurturance, respect, collaboration, and celebration?

What if ... when it was time to evaluate, Jamie's organization was guided by, 'Let's see how the people see the work?'

What if ... Isaac knew where to turn for funding and had an international network of supporters?

What if ... Isaac had the resources he needed to realize his community's vision, and for it to develop on its own terms?

What if ... in the hearts and minds of everyone in the social-good sector, local solutions and grassroots expertise could become respected, envied, even revered?

Prioritize holistic programming

The closer an organization is to the ground, the more connected it is to the community, and the more its leaders are addressing numerous problems at once. To *only* focus on girls' education is a luxury, for example, when you're responding to people in your community. An effective grassroots organization might assess the scenario like this: What does a girl most need to get back into school? Or is she already in school, but struggling with an illness or with family abuse? Who around her is supporting her? What does the family or community need to do to address harmful attitudes or practices towards girls? Does she need help to boost her self-esteem and leadership skills?

When people from your community are knocking on your door for help, you can't say, 'Oh, sorry we don't deal with nutrition or human rights today.' Smart risks are when donors realize that addressing only one issue at a time – and on a short-term, ad hoc basis – will not create lasting change; one programme will not be able to address the totality of factors that keep the girl out of school.

Enable grassroots organizations and movements to remain flexible

Grassroots grant makers should expect good planning; however, they should also look for an organization's capacity to respond and react when things don't go according to plan. Effective grassroots groups are adaptive in the face of a community's arising needs. Not only that – they remain nimble to respond to inherent complexities and local realities of people's lives, and find ingenious ways to advocate for the structural changes needed. This requires donors to creatively restructure and revise their financial controls to make them more 'reality-friendly'.

One way is through providing general operating support to grassroots organizations. This means providing funds with no strings or conditions attached. If they want to pay the light bill, or start a new programme, or plan a demonstration, it's up to them. General operating support does not mean there is no due diligence. It means that a funders' lack of dictates frees up grassroots organizations to listen more closely to the community.

Know that strong programmes require strong operations

Any good businessperson will tell you that investments in personnel and support services are key to success. The same is true for grassroots organizations and movements. Operational costs are fundamental to their survival. This may mean that a donor will not be able to claim, 'my dollar did this', about any one project or specific output. However, how much better to be able to say that by paying the rent, keeping the electricity and the phone/Wi-Fi on, and ensuring people are reimbursed for their expenses, we are contributing to the creation of an empowered organization or movement.

Invest in the best

Grassroots organizations and movements mobilize local resources and use existing social relationships and structures to do their work. This makes them well-placed to ensure maximum utilization of funds and mobilization of people-power.

Effective grassroots organizations are made up of people who understand that a little investment can go a long way in resource-poor settings. It's not always about doing a lot with a little. Seasoned grant makers also know that community-owned initiatives and organizations can do *more with more*. Taking the risk to invest big at an opportune moment can produce even greater returns.

Balance breadth with depth

The amount of funding needed for a child to attend secondary school for a year may be very different to the amount needed for them to visit a nearby health clinic, or for their family to be visited regularly by a local organization's staff member.

Thus easily quantifiable and comparable data, such as cost per beneficiary, are often not useful in drawing comparisons or making conclusions about the effectiveness of different interventions, particularly at the grassroots level. Consider that fundamentally changing the lives of a few children might have a bigger impact than helping many more through a shorter-term activity.

With grassroots grants, think long term

Grassroots grants at the community level have payoffs not just today with services delivered, but also next week, next year, and, hopefully, in decades to come in terms of structures changed and people's rights upheld. Funders of smart risks invest in grassroots leadership, organizations, and movements with a healthy level of uncertainty. They forego potentially short-term returns in favour of lasting outcomes.

A grassroots manifesto

Adapted from the original by Global Fund for Children staff and grantee partners

Around the world, the cutting edge of social change is happening at the grassroots level. Our priority is to make sure this change has every possible chance to grow, to thrive, and to fundamentally disturb the landscape of poverty on this earth.

Grassroots organizations are different – they are the home team. They steadfastly focus on the challenges in their communities because that's what they face every day. They understand the unique needs, resources, and obstacles that surround them.

That's why we are committed to supporting change at the grassroots level. But it's also why grassroots grant making requires a different approach than top-down charity models. On their own, these organizations are small, nimble, tenacious, and inspiring. They are also fragile, and burdened by the very circumstances they are fighting to transform. And their potential to change the world is worth everything we've got.

There are five essentials for excelling in the most exciting philanthropy happening today--and for becoming a true partner at the grassroots.

1. Lead by following

There is no greater expert on a particular community than the community itself. This is not the time for you to direct – this is the time to listen, to support, and to build trust. An indigenous organization may not look like much on the surface. They may not have a business card, or own a permanent office space. But looks can be deceiving, and the best organizations have identified a pressing need in their community and are already working on solutions.

The grassroots organization is just one expert here. So are the people who benefit from the organization's work. When we scout for a new grantee, we walk the neighbourhood with the organization's director. How many people know the director by name or, better yet, invite him or her into their homes? And, even more importantly for us, what do the kids think? During our scouting to find the brightest stars, we've seen where children are the passive recipients of charity, and where they exude childhood joy and agency despite all obstacles. The latter is the real deal.

2. Build trust like it's your job (because it is)

If one of our partners misses a deadline, or experiences a sudden drop in budget, we want to know why – not only for accountability's sake, but also so we can figure out the next step together. Transitions in leadership or the loss of a major funder can dramatically affect a small organization. Because we believe our partners' success is also our own, we do everything we can to help them soften the impact of such setbacks and use these events as learning opportunities.

Grassroots organizations are small, with little bureaucratic experience – maybe they've never even written a grant proposal before. Is the proposal a test or a means to an end? Grassroots grant making is a process that helps organizations to articulate their vision and model and begin to demonstrate their impact. As a true partner, you assist at every step so they can become bigger, stronger, and more sustainable.

Of course, this trust has to be mutual, with accountability structures in place to keep expectations out in the open. Communication is the key, so establishing dialogue (rather than punishment) is the norm.

3. Remove barriers, both large and small

When you're working with grassroots organizations, you'll find no shortage of ground-breaking, awe-inspiring, revolutionary ideas. A funder's role is to remove barriers so those fledgling ideas can take root, grow, and thrive.

Barriers come in all forms. Maybe at first it's the grant proposal itself – so guide people through it. Or maybe what your grantee needs isn't the most glamorous assistance – help them pay rent on their office if that will keep their programmes going, even if it doesn't make a good story for funders. Maybe the organization's director could benefit from attending a conference, but there's no extra cash for that after programme expenses – step in and give them that chance.

An unfortunately common barrier comes in the form of unexpected emergencies. In the developing world, grassroots organizations and the communities they serve are especially vulnerable to natural disaster, war, and civil unrest. It's your job to help your partners do what they do best – so clear the path of whatever might hold them back.

4. Build skills for the long haul

Sustainability is quite the buzzword these days. But when it comes to grassroots grant making, it's the difference between charity and social change. If cash is the only thing you provide to your grantees, you are setting them up to fail after you're gone. The tools that make any organization successful (even your own) are the same tools your partners need – skills in strategic planning, organizational development, human resources, fundraising, and networking. So help your partners run and expand their programmes, but do more than that.

We track our grantees' organizational growth as well as our own impact as a grant maker. Additionally, our grantees build skills in evaluating and addressing their own strengths and weaknesses. We also convene our partners for regional conferences so they can meet, network with, and learn from their peers. We offer special grants for organizational development, and for opportunities like professional training. We tell the world about their leaders, their programmes, and their impact; nominate them for awards; and introduce them to other funders.

These acts are just as important as the cold, hard cash that keeps the lights on. And you'll soon realize they are just as meaningful too.

5. Risk has two sides. Get comfortable with both

Grassroots grant making is built on the premise that nothing important happens in this world until someone takes the first step, however small. Funding under-the-radar organizations demands that you be the first supporter and put your name – and your money – behind what they have courageously begun.

Grassroots grant makers are often the first major US-based funder for our grantees. With more organizational credibility, recognition, and funding, our grantees raise additional dollars from other sources for what we invest.

We have the capacity to invest when others cannot. The task is to know when the risk is worth taking. That means doing your homework: know your partners' leaders, understand their ambitions, walk their neighbourhoods, and keep asking questions. Over the course of the funding relationship, taking smart risks requires appropriate levels of monitoring and reporting, as well as a system for flagging any issues early on. It also means knowing when to stay even though a partner is struggling, and when to leave if the partner is failing.

When you can recognize greatness in its earliest forms and help it to grow into something sustainable, the rewards are incredible. It's not linear – in fact, it's often messy. It's not glamorous, but it has a unique natural beauty.

Witnessing and facilitating this change is both risky *and* smart. And we're here to tell you it's worth it – if you do it well.

The challenge before us now is to become willing to dream big – as grant makers, or giving circles, or social entrepreneurs, or NGO staff, or impact investors, or grassroots leaders, or donors. Those with access to resources can take immediate, paradigm-challenging actions that put power back in the hands of marginalized people and communities. When matched with the vision, resolve, and ingenuity of those coming together all over the world, this model is a proven formula for lasting change.

These are smart risks.

About the authors

Tanya Cothran is executive administrator of Spirit in Action International <http://spiritinaction.org> in California, USA. She lives in Toronto, Canada.

Jennifer Lentfer is director of communications at Thousand Currents (Formerly International Development Exchange – IDEX) <https://www.idex.org> in Berkeley, California, although she is based in Washington DC. She was senior writer of aid effectiveness at Oxfam America from 2012 to 2015, and is the creator of the blog how-matters.org <http://www.how-matters.org>.

Index

Page numbers in *italics* refer to boxes.